What Does Mr. Greenspan *Really* Think?

Alan Greenspan's Speech at the Catholic University Leuven,
Leuven, Belgium January 14, 1997 analyzed by

Lawrence Parks

FAME

**The Foundation for the Advancement of
Monetary Education
New York, NY
www.fame.org**

This publication is designed to provide accurate and
authoritative information in regard to the subject matter
covered. It is sold with the understanding that the publisher
is not engaged in rendering professional services. If
professional advice or other expert assistance is required, the
services of a competent professional should be sought.

Parks, Lawrence M.
    What Does Mr. Greenspan *Really* Think?
    ISBN 0-97-10380-4-X (paper back)

Printed in the U.S. of America
10 9 8 7 6 5 4 3 2 1

"The way our current monetary system works, the careful savings of a lifetime — including your pension — can be wiped out in an eyeblink."

Lawrence Parks

What people are saying about this book:

"With this insightful analysis, Dr. Lawrence Parks reminds us that Daniel Webster was right when he wrote, 'There is nothing so powerful as the truth - and often nothing so strange.' Dr. Lawrence Parks' lucid analysis clearly demonstrates in ordinary language the alarming ways 'What you don't know can hurt you and everyone else, too.' A must read for those who think understanding vital aspects of our nation's monetary policy is beyond them. Do not read this book unless you are ready for several startling monetary truths. Read this book only if you are ready for several jolting truths about the possible threat to our monetary system."

Dr. Amelia Augustus, Ph.D., President
Women's Economic Roundtable

"The logical acuteness of Dr. Parks' commentary on Chairman Alan Greenspan's remarks at the Catholic University Leuvan, Belgium, January 14, 1997, results in the realization to ordinary taxpayers that fiat money is the greatest deception played on humanity since the first enslavement of fellow human beings. Further, even those who understand and acknowledge the hoax being played by Government must cloak the truth with complex words, lest they offend the power brokers (bankers)."

Dominick Attanasio, former President
Societe De Chimie Industrielle

"In *What Does Mr. Greenspan Really Think?*, Larry Parks not only reads between the lines of a Greenspan speech, but also literally writes between them. In doing so, Dr. Parks provides the reader with three vital services: 1) he highlights the discrepancies between what the Fed chairman actually believes and what he is required to do to keep his job; 2) he tears the veil of FedSpeak 'respectability' off of standard operating procedures that are anything but respectable; and, 3) he provides us a primer on what monetary policy really is, how it's run and for whose benefit it's run (hint—not yours and mine). It is quite revealing."

Dr. Robert J. Batemarco, Ph.D.,
Adjunct Assistant Professor of Economics, Marymount College

i

"Were there a bureaucrat controlling any other industry (e.g., farming, fishing, furniture making) who did for it what Alan Greenspan does for monetary policy, we would have no difficulty in labeling him as an economic czar, a socialist of the worst stripe. We would tell him to go back, not to Russia, or East Germany, but to Cuba or North Korea. We would give him Adam Smith's message about the invisible hand being better able to coordinate the activities of millions of people than governmental fiat. But Alan Greenspan, somehow, is different. He is above the fray. He is in effect an economic dictator who widely receives credit as an advocate of free enterprise. He is guilty of the worst excesses of central planning, and is seen by virtually all commentators in the very opposite role. Alan Greenspan has feet of clay; he is an Emperor with no clothes.

Larry Parks is like the small boy who points out the nudity of the king. In this masterful debunking of the Greenspan myth, Dr. Parks places the Chairman of the Board of the Federal Reserve in a well deserved light; not as the savior of the capitalist system, but as one of its greatest enemies."

Dr. Walter Block, Ph.D.
Harold E. Wirth Eminent Scholar
Loyola University New Orleans

"The Federal Reserve System has a profound effect on our daily lives; yet not one in a million truly understands the implications of the Fed's actions and of our monetary structure. This book brings together two people who do understand the system. Alan Greenspan is one such person but is constrained politically from speaking openly about it. Lawrence Parks is another such person who explains Mr. Greenspan's sometimes cryptic and carefully worded remarks in plain English. This book is both a warning and an exposé. The warning is that history has taught us the inherent instability of fiat money. The exposé is of the shocking unfairness of the subsidies involved. Anyone who works for a living or saves for the future should read this book and understand those funny little things called 'dollars.'"

Lloyd Buchanan, Chief Operating Officer
Axe-Haughton Associates, Inc.

"Larry Parks is the shadow public prosecutor who has succeeded in putting Alan Greenspan on the witness stand. The charge is that his Federal Reserve System is not now, nor has it ever been, run in the interest of labor, seniors, or other citizens and taxpayers. On the contrary, it has been run in order to plunder them — as a result of a conspiracy involving Big Banks and Big Government. This unholy alliance has been milking labor and seniors (not to mention widows and orphans) out of their substance for over four scores of years, and their blatant pilfering from savers and taxpayers has pushed our entire economy to the abyss or, in the scholarly words of the witness, 'has exposed the global financial environment to the dangers of a systemic breakdown.' The most amazing thing in all this is the cooperating stance of Dr. Parks' witness. For example, Mr. Greenspan freely admits that 'the central bank [has been given] unlimited power to create money...'. This is tantamount to admitting that, in the United States, the Federal Reserve banks are unconstitutional. That country happens to have a constitution stating in no uncertain terms that it is the charter of a government of *limited* and *enumerated* powers. Not only is the (delegation of) power to create unlimited amounts of money not enumerated, but the *Constitution* explicitly bars the government from letting its bills of credit be organized into currency. Dr. Parks is wondering about the cooperating tone of his witness, too, as the title of his book suggests. While Mr. Greenspan is not testifying under oath, his incentive to speak the truth may be motivated by more powerful considerations. It is the desire to establish a solid public record of eloquent admonitions, in order to cover up his being an accomplice in bringing about a systemic breakdown which, as he might well judge, is by now inevitable. Be that as it may, it would appear incumbent on the suave Mr. Greenspan to initiate a constitutional debate on the monetary provisions of the U.S. *Constitution* which neither he nor his predecessors have ever mustered the decency or the moral courage to recommend for repealing. If he fails to do that, the conclusion remains inescapable that he would rather live with the stigma of violating the *Constitution* every time puts his signature on an official paper, just because labor and seniors appear to be too dumb to understand what's going on. In the meantime, as every discriminating reader of this book will agree, when time comes to put Mr. Greenspan and his accomplices squarely in the dock, the best candidate to act as the *real* prosecutor should be none other than Dr. Parks."

Dr. Antal E. Fekete, Ph.D., Professor Emeritus
Memorial University of Newfoundland

"I have no intention of providing a blurb. I thoroughly disagree."

Professor Milton Friedman, Ph.D.
Winner of the Swedish Bank Prize in Economic Sciences in
Memory of Alfred Nobel, a.k.a., "The Nobel Prize in Economics"

"Reading Lawrence Parks' study of Alan Greenspan's analysis of contemporary economics, one encounters approbation of the gold standard and phenomena such as fiat money, inflation, volatile interest rates, evanescent safety nets, moral callousness, pernicious transfers of wealth, undeserved rewards and unjust punishments. It is lucid and frightening, and a stern and principled critique of the financial architecture of our economy. Whether or not one agrees with its call for a recrudescence of the gold standard, the reader will be educated and perforce, outraged. This potent plea is a monetary equivalent of Tom Paine's 'The Crisis.'"

Murray I. Franck, Esq. Law Professor,
City University of New York

"Mr. Parks presents real food for thought relating to the issue of fiscal responsibility."

Jack Gargan
Former National Chairman of the Reform Party

"By analyzing an Alan Greenspan talk in Belgium January 14,1997, Larry Parks presents a devastating critique of Federal Reserve policy. The Fed tries to maintain a precarious balance betwixt the Scylla of implosion (economic collapse) and the Charybdis of inflation. On the one hand Greenspan admits that the Fed's 'unlimited power to create money' 'induces' banks to expand credit and make potentially risky loans. A 'safety net/subsidy' then protects the banks from losses on bad loans even though, as Greenspan admits, the subsidy distorts incentives by relieving banks of the full costs of the risks taken and, if regularly anticipated, 'would only encourage reckless and irresponsible practices.' Moreover, Parks explains, the 'safety/net subsidy' benefits banks, at the expense of taxpayers, workers and seniors. On the other hand, if the Fed allowed bank loans to default, a chain reaction might set in, 'culminat[ing] in financial implosion.'

Because 'market signals that usually accompany excessive risk-taking are substantially muted,' as a result of Fed policy, 'and because the prices to banks of government deposit guarantees . . . do not, and probably cannot, vary sufficiently with risk to mimic market prices,' central bank officials 'try to achieve the proper balance through official regulations, as well as through formal and informal supervisory policies and procedures.' In the process, they 'are compelled to act as a surrogate for market discipline.' Central bank officials, who are no less fallible than other human beings, cannot possibly know 'what market responses. . . would occur if there were no safety net.' Yet they make decisions every day, either explicitly or by default, that affect the lives of everyone. And Fed Chairman Greenspan admits that he and his colleagues 'can never know for sure whether the decisions [they] made were appropriate.'

On the one hand the Fed seeks to employ with caution its unlimited power to create money so as not to induce over-expansion, and on the other hand it tries to mute the effect on prices of its subsidizing of risky bank loans. And at the same time it pursues an impossible dream — of trying to replicate market prices. Parks describes Fed policy not only as one fraught with danger, but also as absolutely unnecessary if we should adopt gold as money and leave to private lenders the right to make loans without fear of government threat or favor."

Dr. Bettina Bien Greaves, Ph.D.
Resident Scholar, The Foundation for Economic Education

"Dr. Parks portrays Alan Greenspan as a central planner, *par excellence.* In his scholarly analysis of the Fed Chairman's own words, he exposes an important truth about the Western World's financial system....that it is nothing more than a confection held together by the decisions and judgments of this very fallible individual and his co-central planners, the Fed Governors. It is hard to conclude after reading this commentary that the system is on sound footing. In fact, it has been built upon ever more reckless interventions into freely trading markets which by Greenspan's own words have distorted incentives and increased the leverage of its core financial institutions."

John Hathaway, CFA, Senior Partner
Tocqueville Asset Management, LP

v

"Who is Alan Greenspan? Why do we care what he thinks? What the hell is he saying, and why in the world do we ordinary citizens and working stiffs let him keep robbing us? Larry Parks tells all. Read, reflect, rebel."

Jim Hightower
Author, America's #1 Populist

"Alan Greenspan is highly regarded on Wall Street. But he has one severe critic: Alan Greenspan. Larry Parks has the ability to translate Mr. Greenspan's statements into common sense English, and this reveals the enormous gulf between what Mr. Greenspan <u>says</u> and what he is <u>doing</u>. Given the great power that Mr. Greenspan has over the U.S. economy, it is very disturbing that this man is suffering a crisis of conscience over his own behavior. Since so much in our lives depends on him, *What Does Mr. Greenspan <u>Really</u> Think?* is a must read for anyone who wishes to understand the world in which he lives."

Howard S. Katz, Author
<u>The Paper Aristocracy</u>

"In a rational society, Alan Greenspan would earn a living in some useful pursuit like pumping gas or flipping burgers. Larry Parks would be systematically dismantling the Federal Reserve System and they would both benefit from the increased prosperity that this reallocation of responsibilities would bring about."

Robert D. Kephart

"After two relevant degrees from Harvard and a lifetime career involving money, I feel that *What Does Mr. Greenspan <u>Really</u> Think?* ranks with the best of books of this genre both as to readability and insight. I pray it receives widespread attention and that Dr. Parks' views as to the inequities and misallocation of resource attributable to fiat money be brought into the public debate."

Hon. Brewster Kopp
Former Assistant Secretary of the Army (Financial Management)
Former principal financial officer, First National Bank of Boston

"Dr. Parks' book is a must for anybody interested in the world of finance and the future of human society. Mr. Alan Greenspan who, in his younger years, was one of the most eloquent proponents and defenders of 'Gold and Economic Freedom,' has become prisoner of an unholy system and has betrayed his earlier convictions. Today, he seems like a shaman who gets his message from the gods of evil, and he speaks in symbolic language only understood by the initiated few. Damned be the man on the street, the workers, the pensioners and the economically weak. All who do not know history are condemned to repeat it. France's experience with John Law is being repeated today on a worldwide basis. But, Dr. Parks has learned his lesson well. He demonstrates that the only way out of this avalanche of misallocations leading to the complete destruction of the world economy is the gold standard. He prods us into the realization that the only currency that can lead the world back to prosperity, justice, order, culture and peace is gold."

Ferdinand Lips
Private Banker, Switzerland

"There are very few people who understand the arcane ways in which money is created or, for that matter, who benefits and who is adversely affected by this act of creation. By parsing the language of the Fed chairman, Larry Parks has uncovered a minefield of illuminating observations. Larry Parks, the president of FAME, is the quintessential truth-teller in a world of obscurantism and misunderstanding. For most people, banking and global finance are a mystery wrapped in an enigma. However, the creation of fiat money affects transactions, buying power, investments, personal wealth and the rise and fall of nation states. Even today the runaway inflation during the German Weimar period in the 1930's affects the attitude of the European Central bankers. Through textual analysis Mr. Parks offers extraordinary insight into the operation of the Federal Reserve and, as importantly, the future purchasing power of money. Lest anyone think these are either abstract or pettifogging matters, the creation of money is a transfer of wealth from Mr. and Mrs. John Q. Public to the banking establishment. It is hard to conceive of any issue that is more profound than this one."

Dr. Herbert I. London, Ph.D., President
Hudson Institute

"*What Does Mr. Greenspan Really Think?* is dynamite! Mr. Greenspan has really spilled the beans, and Dr. Parks has caught him red-handed. In effect, Mr. Greenspan's assertion that the Federal Reserve stands ready to create money 'without limit' is in fact an admission that none of us have any property rights in anything denominated in 'dollars,' including our savings, our stock portfolios, and our pensions. The reason is that those 'rights' can be diluted to nothing to bail out the banking system on account of banks leveraging their balance sheets to garner ever-greater unearned profits! It is certainly a credit to Mr. Greenspan that he has opened the door to the issue of ordinary taxpayers subsidizing the banks, and, as Dr. Parks has shown, what a subsidy that is! How else to explain the more than $600 billion that the financial sector takes out of the economy? I am in awe of what is being said, and I am dismayed that the establishment media has not focused on this. This book is a real eye-opener. Dr. Parks has done an important public service by writing it."

Dan Mahony

"Dr. Parks has accomplished the equivalent of a headline 'scoop,' but for academicians and those with a longer term view on the important factors affecting our world and our lives. The Fed, its chairmen, and Alan Greenspan in particular are not known for straightforward clarity. Indeed, Mr. Greenspan's actions often seem to contradict the economic principles he espouses. He does a superb job of obfuscation—of keeping domestic analysts and reporters perplexed regarding his actual beliefs and the principles on which he bases the decisions that affect all our lives significantly. Offshore, freed from the scrutiny of domestic observers, Mr. Greenspan uncharacteristically let his guard down. Apparently he did not reckon with the likes of Dr. Lawrence Parks. Dr Parks has, for once and all, defined for us many of Alan Greenspan's economic principles in clear, unambiguous terms for the first time, with irrefutable logic applied to 'best evidence,' straight from the horse's mouth. This is an inestimable service to all who need or want to understand the mindset and motivations of the man at the helm of our banking system, whose decisions determine our collective economic destiny. Mr. Greenspan is a man who understands much more than he lets on—but who is apparently willing and even eager at times to act in diametric opposition to his own professed beliefs. If you are an acute

Fed observer, Dr. Parks will confirm with irrefutable evidence much of what you may have heretofore only suspected—and you may well discover a few surprises in his analysis too."

Morris Markovitz, Author, President
Mercury Asset Management Corp

"What Does Mr. Greenspan Really Think?" by Dr. Lawrence Parks is an interesting, thorough and rational analysis of our monetary system as managed by the Federal Reserve. It should be read by professionals who are involved as economists, bankers, experts interested in the U.S. economy, and by lay persons who will be affected by the action or lack of action of the banking community. I am somewhat amazed by my belief that even among the experts there is little understanding or acceptance of the implications of Dr. Parks' explanation of Mr. Greenspan's comments about our monetary system."

Herbert S. Meeker, Esq., Partner
Baer Marks & Upham

"There is good research, provocative disclosure, and much food for thought in Dr. Parks' erudite analysis of 'Doc' Greenspan's speech."

Dr. Victor Niederhoffer, Ph.D.
Speculator, Author, World Champion squash player

"Lawrence Parks has written an insightful book about the most powerful man in the world. If you have any money — you need to read this book."

Bill O'Reilly, Television Anchor
Author, The O'Reilly Factor

"My old friend Larry Parks has done the nation a valuable service by exposing how even Alan Greenspan, the 'man behind the curtain' in America's monetary OZ, knows that the Federal Reserve is an unaccountable bureaucracy that enriches special interests at the expense of working Americans and our nation's economic security. I highly recommend this work to anyone who wishes to understand the dangers of our fiat money system and the reforms necessary to ensure the dollar is once again 'as good as gold.'"

Hon. Ron Paul, MD
Member of the United States House of Representatives
Member of the House Banking Committee

"Larry Parks has performed an extraordinary public service by explaining with clarity in layman's language the ways and means by which Congress has permitted the Federal Reserve System to tax the American people without any real accountability to either Congress or the taxpayers. Using direct quotes from Alan Greenspan, Parks demonstrates how the earnings and savings of the American people have been diminished to enrich a powerful Establishment elite. My prayer is that our President, our Vice President, and every member of Congress will take the time to read this book, and that perhaps some few of them will understand it and even act on it."

Howard Phillips, Chairman
The Conservative Caucus

"In *What Does Mr. Greenspan Really Think?* Larry Parks has translated the Orwellian 'newspeak' of the Federal Reserve into language understandable by us all. Anyone who reads Dr. Parks' hard-hitting translation of Alan Greenspan's words will never again fall victim to the irrational belief that the Federal Reserve is the guardian of the national economy. His book is a great addition to the literature on sound money."

John A. Pugsley
Chairman, The Sovereign Society

"How refreshing it is to read a clear-headed, critical analysis of the Federal Reserve and its operations, as opposed to the official news releases the major media is happy to regurgitate without serious question! One doesn't have to agree with every point Dr. Parks makes to realize that he has performed a valuable public service by explaining in lay terms why the monetary emperor has no clothes."

Dr. Lawrence W. Reed, Ph.D. President
Mackinac Center for Public Policy

"It's great to see Greenspan deconstructed, as only Larry Parks could do."

Llewellyn H. Rockwell, Jr., President
Ludwig Von Mises Institute

"Finally, someone tells us what Mr. Greenspan really thinks! Dr. Lawrence Parks gives Americans the first penetrating insights into a man who has tremendous influence on all of our lives. I encourage you to read *What Does Mr. Greenspan Really Think?*"

Christopher Ruddy, President & CEO
NewsMax.com

"This book is like a 1773 Thomas Paine pamphlet calling for freedom. Freedom from Greenspan and what he represents. The need is as desperate as it was in 1773. We need to get this book into the hands of innocent citizens."

Chevalier Harry D. Schultz
International Harry Schultz Letter

"Larry Parks is like a sculptor who chips away at a rough-hewn block of marble until he reveals the art work 'hidden' inside. Only here there is a gargoyle waiting within the marble, because Parks' raw material is the elusive mind that lurks behind the familiar, impassive countenance of Alan Greenspan. This man, the most powerful figure in the realms of money, banking, and finance, discusses central banks and their effects on economic conditions. In ruthless fashion, Parks analyzes Greenspan's remarks and translates them into common language. What one finds is that the combination of central banking and fiat currency is a deadly one. Modern monetary systems encourage excessive risk-taking by financial intermediaries, can create crippling rates of inflation, and, above all, redistribute part of the wealth and income of the average taxpayer to a politically-privileged elite. The solution? Get rid of the bureaucratic management and return to the market discipline imposed by *laissez-faire* principles and a gold standard. I could not agree more."

Dr. Larry J. Sechrest, Ph.D.
Associate Professor of Economics
Sul Ross State University

"Understanding the actual workings of our monetary system is very complicated for most people including myself. Money to the economy is like air to a living organism; it is necessary. Do we have the right kind of money? Larry Parks does an amazing job at making our system understandable and creates reading that every American can and should comprehend."

Denison E. Smith, Chairman, For Our Grandchildren

"In conventional wisdom, economics is the dismal science and Fed Chairman Alan Greenspan is the saintly, obscure master regulator of our nation's and the world's economic well being. Dr. Larry Parks, in a unique and challenging intellectual *tour de force*, makes economics anything but dismal and Chairman Greenspan anything but obscure. This volume is worth reading for fun or, if one prefers, for profit and understanding. *What Does Mr. Greenspan Really Think?* is not to be taken lightly because the implications of what is revealed are truly momentous. The very heart of this nation's economic system, fiat money, is an intricate contrivance which is inherently unstable and unfair. Our apparent success to date says more about the astuteness of the Chairman than it does about the suitability of the system. We are proceeding at breakneck speed and at enormous risk, gambling all the while on good luck and human perfection. Neither one can be assured with confidence. This book is an understandable call to arms."

Charles Darwin Snelling,
Columnist, MCALL.com; Venture Capitalist

"We should all be thankful that Mr. Greenspan has raised the issues of financial collapse, ongoing wealth transfer from ordinary citizens to the banking system, and, especially, that the banking system has a call on virtually all of everyone's savings and promises of future payment—such as pensions—by virtue of the Federal Reserve's mandated function to create money without limit to attempt to quell a systemic collapse. But we should be even more thankful that Dr. Parks has brilliantly translated Mr. Greenspan's arcane language into a form that everyone can understand. *What Does Mr. Greenspan Really Think?* is essential reading for anyone who is concerned about their investment portfolio and, more important, justice, fairness and living in a just society."

Dr. Leon Sutton, Ph.D.,Abraham Ben Jacob Sutton Foundation

"Larry Parks has laid bare the essence of the monetary system and it should scare the wits out of you. Not only is our economic system based on the flimsiest of reeds—fiat money—but, as such, it rewards the idle at the expense of hard-working Americans, and people the world over."

Greg Tarpinian, Executive Director
Labor Research Association

"This little book is wonderful. By providing an insightful analysis of a major speech delivered by Alan Greenspan, Dr. Lawrence Parks has created an educational tool of great use. Reading between the lines and translating arcane jargon into terms everyone can understand, Dr. Parks identifies the fallacies, myths and the ultimate folly of central banking and its diabolical progeny: fiat currency. I hope that this book is circulated wide and far so that many people are given the opportunity to read not only what central banks have done to our money, but what they have done to our society — in other words, what they have done to us."

James Turk, Managing Director & Founder
GoldMoney

"In *What Does Mr. Greenspan Really Think?* Dr. Lawrence Parks brilliantly translates and deconstructs the latest Greenspanese— demonstrating that the Federal Reserve System's true purpose is to employ *fiat* currency and bank credit to redistribute real wealth from average citizens to an economic and political elite. Moreover, that the Federal Reserve can, as Chairman Greenspan admits, 'produce [fiat] money without limit,' means that it can redistribute society's wealth just as thoroughly—implying that no one outside the elite can enjoy economic security as long as the central bank exists. So, Dr. Parks' commentary is both an education and a warning that all Americans need to study, to take to heart, and to act upon before the harsh laws of economics call the Federal Reserve System to account."

Dr. Edwin Vieira, Jr., Esq., President & Founder
National Alliance Constitutional Money

"Most will recall the childhood game called 'telephone' whereby a message is passed from person to person, and then, at the end of the chain, the message turns out to be greatly distorted from its original content. In the media today, that describes what generally happens to Mr. Greenspan's remarks. Dr. Parks has short-circuited this process by juxtaposing Mr. Greenspan's comments with what they mean in plain English so that ordinary people can understand his message, and that message is very profound. In this small and very important book, Dr. Parks raises questions that should be the concern everyone, and especially our elected representatives. As the former President of the New York Chapter of the Federalist Society, I can say with some authority that *What Does Mr. Greenspan Really Think?* should be studied by every citizen. It is a truly remarkable and valuable accomplishment."

Michael Weinberger, Esq.
Former President, Federalist Society – NY Chapter

"Straight talk from a straight shooter."
Kathryn M. Welling, Editor and Publisher
Welling@Weeden, Weeded & Co. LP

"The most important aspect of this extraordinary book is the basic question it raises: Is the power Mr. Greenspan wields consistent with our system of limited constitutional government? Dr. Parks' thoughtful analysis and easy-to-understand explanation of Mr. Greenspan's views should be at the top of the agenda of anyone concerned about his economic future."

Hon. Faith Whittlesey, President & Chairman
American Swiss Foundation
Former U.S. Ambassador to Switzerland

About Lawrence Parks

Lawrence Parks is the Executive Director of the Foundation for the Advancement of Monetary Education (FAME). He has broad experience in academia, in business, and in finance.

He holds a Ph.D. in Operations Research from the Polytechnic University. Dr. Parks has studied the money issue for more than thirty years. His writings have appeared in *Pensions & Investments*, *The Economist*, *The Washington Times*, *The Freeman*, *The Free Market*, *American Outlook*, *The United States Congressional Record*, *National Review*, and others.

He is an active member of many civic and social organizations, a member of The United Association for Labor Education, The National Writer's Union, UAW 1981, AFL-CIO, and he is a frequent speaker on the Fight for Honest Monetary Weights and Measures.

His focus is on how our present fiat monetary system operates to destroy savings, pensions and jobs and what to do about it.

Table of Contents

Foreword

by

Lawrence Parks

Mr. Greenspan is the most brilliant of anyone who has ever served at the Federal Reserve. I have found some of his speeches, especially those given out of the country, to be extraordinarily candid about the perils—such as possible systemic collapse—of our irredeemable-paper-ticket-checkbook (fiat) money system and, alternatively, the benefits of the gold standard.

Mr. Greenspan is careful with his language. Sometimes he makes straightforward assertions that he believes to be true. Interspersed with these are statements that he qualifies with words such as "presumably," "possibly as a consequence," and so on. In these cases, I believe he is signaling that he does not share this position. Otherwise, he would leave out the qualifier.

The position he holds as Federal Reserve Chairman constrains his language. At the end of his speech, he says that he has to operate within the "context of his political environment." I take this to mean that he does not see himself as someone who can boldly oppose or overtly criticize the current system. However, he is doing us a huge service by repeatedly emphasizing the disaster that awaits us with our present fiat monetary system and the benefits that we would enjoy with gold-as-money.

Mr. Greenspan has pointed the way. It is up to us to use the intellectual ammunition he has provided. It's a mystery to me why the press and others are not paying more attention to what he's been saying repeatedly for the past three years or more. Perhaps the reason lies with his arcane language.

To help explain how our monetary system works and make Mr. Greenspan's views more easily understood, I have: (1) translated his FedSpeak terminology into plain English; (2) added critical comments; and, (3) suggested areas where further explanation ought to be forthcoming. Where I believe he is mistaken, I say so.

In effect, by enlarging upon Mr. Greenspan's statements, I have constructed a primer about how our monetary system works to transfer wealth from poorer people (ordinary taxpayers) to richer people (bankers and those with a stake in Wall Street firms).

Lawrence Parks, Executive Director

Foundation for the Advancement of Monetary Education

July 24, 1999

Revised: July 30, 2001

Key Issues Raised by Federal Reserve Chairman Alan Greenspan and discussed and analyzed by Lawrence Parks:

1 - Ordinary taxpayers subsidize banks.

By the Federal Reserve's providing a "lender of last resort (bailout) facility" safety net to banks (and possibly other financial institutions) in the event that they experience catastrophic losses, ordinary taxpayers subsidize banks.[1] Because every subsidy involves wealth transfer by definition, this means that ordinary taxpayers are transferring wealth to bankers. Mr. Greenspan is very explicit that the safety net for banks is in fact a subsidy.

2 - Government guarantees induce banks to increase risk.

Relying on government's guarantee to make up catastrophic losses they may experience, banks are, using Mr. Greenspan's word, "induced" to take more risks than they would otherwise. They do this by increasing leverage. Mr. Greenspan calls this "moral hazard." In fact, the principal purpose of the Federal Reserve is to mute deleveraging when losses occur.

3 - The Federal Reserve harms ordinary working people.

When it perceives that banks are engaging in too much leverage, the Federal Reserve "signals" banks by manipulating interest rates higher. In Mr. Greenspan's words, "interest rates are allowed to rise." This works to the disadvantage of ordinary working people because higher interest rates tend to snuff out jobs.

4 - The Federal Reserve puts the entire economy at risk.

Increased leverage makes the banking system—and by implication our monetary system and our entire economy—vulnerable to a systemic breakdown, a complete collapse. In the U.S., if the Federal Reserve is called upon to bail out the banks, the Federal Reserve may create money "without limit" to do so. In Mr. Greenspan's words, "... if central banks effectively insulate private institutions from the largest potential losses, however incurred, increased laxity *could threaten a major drain on taxpayers or produce inflationary instability as a consequence of excess money creation.*" [Emphasis added.] The

1

direction of this "major drain"—wealth transfer—is clearly from ordinary taxpayers to the "private institutions" the Federal Reserve is "insulating": banks and other financial sector firms. No other segment of society receives these guarantees or special privileges.

5 - Mr. Greenspan concedes lack of knowledge.

To help preclude such a collapse, which Mr. Greenspan believes the Federal Reserve can accomplish with a "high probability," but not a certainty, the Federal Reserve attempts to regulate banks by somehow mimicking the market. While Mr. Greenspan says that the Federal Reserve cannot be certain that it is making correct decisions, at least one other former member of the Board of Governors (Larry Lindsey) conceded that the Federal Reserve has no special knowledge and puzzles why anyone would think otherwise.

6 - Mr. Greenspan says gold-as-money solves these problems.

If our monetary system were based on gold-as-money, then there would be less leveraging by banks and other financial institutions. Banks would make bets with their own money and would bear the complete risk of loss. Under these conditions, the risk of a total financial collapse would be, in Mr. Greenspan's words, "virtually eliminated." At the same time, interest rates would be lower, there would be no need for taxpayers to subsidize banks, no wealth transfer, and no inflation. This sounds good to me.

7 - All of our money is fiat (arbitrary).

The money in our society and around the world is all fiat; it is created out of thin air by banks and by the Fed. Since 1947, banks in the U.S. have created almost $7 *trillion*.

> Note: Perhaps for emphasis, Mr. Greenspan repeats himself, sometimes several times. Because my explanations track his language, I have repeated myself as well. I have placed particular focus on the effects of our monetary system on ordinary working people and seniors, since they are the principal victims of our fiat money monetary system.

Lawrence Parks

Remarks by Chairman Alan Greenspan
At the Catholic University Leuven, Leuven, Belgium
January 14, 1997

Annotations by Lawrence Parks are in **Arial 14pt type** to distinguish them from those of Chairman Greenspan.

Central Banking and Global Finance

Mr. Prime Minister, Minister of Finance, Minister of Budget, Rector Oosterlinck, Professor Peeters, ladies and gentlemen, it is a distinct honor, and a great personal pleasure, to be here today to receive this degree from such a distinguished and historic university. Central bankers, because of the continuity of our institutions and the nature of our responsibilities, typically are said to take a long-term view. By that, I mean we try to look beyond the current calendar quarter to the next year or maybe even a few years beyond.

A drawback of irredeemable-paper-ticket or electronic-checkbook (fiat) money is that it shortens the investment-time-horizon.[2] Because fiat money is created out of nothing and because there is no limit on how much can be created, there is risk that fiat money paid in the future will have uncertain purchasing power. To mitigate this risk, the future is truncated. It's significant that Mr. Greenspan thinks that the long term is "next year" or "maybe even a few years beyond." This is different from what most generally consider the long term.

Standing here in this university, which was founded more than 500 years ago and had already become a leading university in Europe by the 16th century, gives a meaningful perspective to what central bankers consider the longer term.

Today, I shall address the various roles of a central bank encompassing: bank supervision, the provision of financial services, and, of course, monetary policy. I recognize that not all central banks are the same, and in particular that the central bank's role in bank supervision varies considerably from one country to another. However, I view these three elements of a central bank's responsibilities as closely interrelated and mutually supporting, in ways that I will endeavor to elaborate.

Before doing so, I might note that the global financial environment in which central banks operate has become an increasingly important factor in carrying out our responsibilities. This is obviously true of smaller and more open economies like Belgium, but it is true also of countries like the United States that are sometimes thought to be self-contained. Monetary policy in all countries must take account of its effects on, and feedback from, the rest of the world. Many financial services provided by central banks involve cross-border transactions of one kind or another. These international relationships add still one more degree of complexity to the already complex lives of central bankers. That is one of our challenges.

One of the rewards is the international cooperation that these complexities have spawned. That process of cooperation has been especially deep and long-standing among central banks of the G-10 countries, but it involves finance ministries and officials from other agencies and other countries, as well. I call this one of the rewards not just because it has enhanced the policy process but also, on a more personal level, because it has enabled me to develop good friendships with many of my counterparts, including Alfons Verplaetse of the National Bank of Belgium.

Let me begin with the fundamental observation, that a nation's sovereign credit rating **[a nation's ability to borrow]** lies at the base of its current fiscal, monetary, and, indirectly, regulatory policy.

When there is confidence in the integrity of government, monetary authorities—the central bank and the finance ministry—can issue unlimited claims [create out of nothing an unlimited amount of money] denominated in their own currencies and can guarantee or stand ready to guarantee the obligations [debts] of private issuers [private borrowers] as they see fit. This power has profound implications for both good and ill for our economies.[3]

It is an abuse of power for a government agency to "guarantee" or "stand ready to guarantee" debts of a unique group of private borrowers which, in this case, consists of politically-connected bankers and Wall Street firms. Because there is a cost associated with any guarantee, this means that ordinary taxpayers are subsidizing banks. Later in this speech, Mr. Greenspan explicitly declares this to be the case.

Mr. Greenspan is mistaken when he says that some of the implications may be good for our economies. They are all bad. Tellingly, he doesn't mention any of the implications.

Central banks can issue currency [create money out of nothing], a non-interest-bearing claim on the government, effectively without limit. They can discount loans and other assets of banks or other private depository institutions, thereby converting potentially illiquid private assets into riskless claims on the government in the form of deposits at the central bank.[4]

A "claim on the government" misstates the case. The money created out of nothing is irredeemable—just ink on paper or "electronic-checkbook" money. Because there is no redeemability, there can be no claim for anything, just a *potential* claim.

A "potentially illiquid private asset" is something that cannot be sold at par, e.g., it may be worthless. So, here we have the Federal Reserve possibly buying potentially worthless "loans and other assets" from an exclusive group of private companies and paying for them with money that the Federal Reserve creates.

To "discount loans" refers to loans that may be in default, e.g., the borrower may be broke and the loan may be worthless. In this case, the Federal Reserve may purchase the loan for less than its face value, i.e., "discount" it, and pay for it with money which it creates. Further, the Federal Reserve may create that money, in Mr. Greenspan's words, "effectively without limit."

"Other assets" may be anything, e.g., real estate or stocks that a bank has purchased. For example, suppose a bank lent $1 billion to Russia (or Mexico or a hedge fund or another bank) and the borrower could not or would not repay the loan. Instead of booking a loss and writing off the loan, the bank could possibly "sell" the loan to the Fed, presumably at a discount (which could be no discount at all).[5] When the Federal Reserve pays for what it buys, it literally creates the money out of thin air, diluting the purchasing power of money already in circulation and that which has been promised for future payment, such as pensions.

Fundamentally, this is no different from counterfeiting, except that it is being done by a quasi-government agency for the benefit of a particular group of citizens (usually bankers). We can take little comfort that the Federal Reserve does not do this often. Knowing that there is a "lender of last resort" induces banks to make "investments" and bets that they would not make if they had to bear the complete risk of loss. Mr. Greenspan later describes this as "moral hazard."

That all of these claims on government are readily accepted reflects the fact that a government cannot become insolvent with respect to obligations in its own currency. *A fiat money system, like the ones we have today,* can produce such claims [dollars] *without limit.* [Emphasis added.]

It is crucial to understand what fiat money is. FAME Foundation Scholar Edwin Vieira has it exactly right:

". . . a fiat money is a medium of exchange composed of some intrinsically valueless substance which the issuer does *not* promise to redeem in a commodity or a fiduciary money. Because a fiat money has no direct legal connexion to a commodity money (in terms of redemption) and, therefore, no real economic cost to its production, the supply of a fiat money can never be self-limiting; and the value of a fiat money is always largely a matter of public confidence in the economic or political stability of the issuer. For these reasons, historically almost all fiat monies have self-destructed in what is popularly called "hyperinflation" (that is, extreme decreases in the purchasing-power) caused by either unlimited increases in the supply of those fiat monies by the issuers or accelerating loss of public confidence in the continued value of the money or economic or political fortunes of their issuers, or both."[6]

Thus, one reason why all fiat monetary systems collapse is because conditions arise, such as the need to bail out banks, that cause central banks to create too much fiat money. Mr. Greenspan's five repetitions in this speech that central banks may create money "without limit" demonstrate his concern. I take it as a warning.

Former Federal Reserve Chairman Paul Volcker has also warned us:

> "The truly unique power of a central bank, after all, is the power to create money, and ultimately the power to create is the power to destroy."[7]

To be sure, if a central bank produces too many [if it creates too much fiat money], inflation will inexorably rise as will interest rates, and economic activity will inevitably be constrained by the misallocation of resources induced by inflation.

As fiat money is created in the limit, it is said to "melt," interest rates go to double or triple digits, the purchasing power of savings are destroyed, the value of future payments such as pensions become worthless, workers lose their jobs, commercial obligations predicated upon future payment unravel, and the economy implodes. This scenario is now slowly unfolding in South Korea, Indonesia, Malaysia, Russia and elsewhere. If we continue with fiat money, why shouldn't the same fate await us? As Andrew Smithers writes concerning the genesis of the Asian currency crisis:

". . . we need to understand what went wrong.
Stanley Fischer of the International Monetary Fund
believes Asian countries made three key policy
mistakes. First, they allowed their economies to
become overheated, as shown by their large
external deficits and asset price bubbles. Second,
they borrowed too much from abroad and third, their
banks lent badly. No other countries should,
therefore, allow themselves to get into a similar
mess. Unfortunately they already have. The U.S.
has a large external deficit, the biggest stock market
bubble in its history, huge overseas borrowing and a
record level of bankruptcies."[8]

If it produces too few, the economy's expansion also will *presumably*
be constrained by a shortage of the necessary lubricant for transactions.
Authorities must struggle continuously to find the proper balance.
[Emphasis added.]

I suspect the qualifier "presumably" means that Mr.
Greenspan doesn't believe this is necessarily true. If he
did, he would have omitted this word.

It was not always thus. For most of the period prior to the early 1930s,
obligations of governments in major countries were payable in gold.
This meant the whole outstanding debt of government was subject to
redemption in a medium **[gold]**, the quantity of which could not be
altered at the will of government. Hence, debt issuance and budget
deficits were constrained by the potential market response to an
inflated economy.

Mr. Greenspan is explaining that benefits of gold-as-
money include: (1) less debt; and, (2) we would not
have continuing budget deficits. There would be no

need for a "Balanced Budget Amendment" or any special action by the Congress to balance the budget.

If politicians sought to borrow too much money, interest rates would increase, private borrowers such as manufacturers, entrepreneurs, and home buyers would complain, and spending and concomitant borrowing would be reduced. This is consistent with the position Mr. Greenspan took in 1966. Then, he wrote:

> ". . . the gold standard is incompatible with chronic deficit spending (the hallmark of the welfare state)."[9]

It was even possible in such a monetary regime for a government to become insolvent.

The threat of government insolvency is actually a benefit. It provides discipline to politicians and prevents them from spending taxpayer money with abandon. Without this constraint, banks and the Federal Reserve may create an unlimited amount of money which politicians have ready access to. As a result, with a fiat monetary system, there are no bounds on what politicians may attempt to do. If they don't have to tax citizens to pay for their programs but can, instead, have access to newly-created money in unlimited quantities, they have in effect a claim on all of the accumulated wealth of the country.

Creating an unlimited amount of fiat money is not a power to which the Federal Reserve is entitled under the *Constitution* nor one which citizens should want it to have. Also, it was not a power anticipated as part of the original enabling legislation that brought the Federal Reserve into being. Somehow, after the camel got its nose under the tent, it went into the tent. Similarly, one may recall a comment made by famed actress Zsa Zsa Gabor who, while explaining the circumstances of her first sexual encounter, said that her partner enticed her by promising to put in no more than the tip of his finger.

Indeed, the United States skirted on the edges of bankruptcy in 1895 when our government gold stock shrank ominously and was bailed out by a last minute gold loan, underwritten by a Wall Street syndicate.

"Bailed out" is the wrong terminology. There was no wealth transfer. The Wall Street syndicate was fully secured, and there was no fiat money.

There is little doubt that under the gold standard the restraint on both public and private credit creation limited price inflation, but it was also increasingly perceived as too restrictive to government discretion.

Until the U.S. adopted fiat money, inflation was never a big problem. As the Federal Reserve Bank of Richmond teaches:

> "When the Federal Reserve was established in 1913, inflation was not the problem it was to become in the latter part of the century. The nation was on the gold standard and the purchasing power of money in 1913 was about what it had been 30 years before, or for that matter, 100 years before. The gold standard sharply restricted inflation by requiring that money created by the U.S. Treasury be backed by gold."[10]

While Mr. Greenspan is correct about the gold standard limiting price inflation, further explanation is warranted. Under the gold standard, there is generally moderate price *deflation* as manufacturers acquire intellectual and physical capital and as workers' skills increase. The result is that the quality of goods and services improve, prices decrease, and the quantity of goods and services increase. This is what an increasing standard of living means: more and better goods and services for more people at cheaper prices. This was the experience in the United States after President Grant signed the Resumption Legislation in 1874 and the U.S. went back on the gold standard after the Civil War.

Also, limiting government discretion is desirable. The historical record shows only too clearly that, when politicians and central bankers are in charge of the integrity of fiat money, they have never been able to resist the temptation to manipulate the fiat money for their own benefit. They have always driven its value to its cost of production—which is near zero.

The abandonment of the domestic convertibility of gold effectively augmented the power of the monetary authorities to create claims. ["To create claims" means to create money out of nothing.] Possibly as a consequence, post-World War II fluctuations in gross domestic product have been somewhat less than those prior to the 1930s, and no major economic contraction of the dimensions experienced in earlier years has occurred in major industrial countries. [Here, again, Mr. Greenspan uses the qualifier word "possibly" to signal that he may not believe this. He is careful with his language. If he thought that creating money out of nothing were beneficial, he would have left out the word "possibly."] On the other hand, peace-time inflation has been far more virulent.

Inflation, which is the consequence of creating money out of nothing, constitutes stealing from seniors, ordinary working people, and others. Banks, Wall Street firms, large credit-worthy borrowers, and politicians benefit, at least in the short run. Everyone else loses. Creating money out of nothing dilutes the value of money saved and money promised for future payment, such as workers' pensions.

Today, the widespread presumption is that, as a consequence of expectations of continuing inflation over the longer run, both nominal and real long-term interest rates are currently higher than they would otherwise be. Arguably, at root is the potential, however remote, of unconstrained issuance of claims [the "unconstrained creation of money out of nothing"] unsupported by the production of goods and services and the accumulation of real assets. [I cannot be certain why he refers to money creation as the "issuance of claims." Near the end of this speech he lapses into clarity and talks about the "creation of money without limit."][11]

The potential "unconstrained issuance" of money is not "remote" for two reasons. First, a good case can be made that the viability of our monetary system has become much more unstable and it is much closer to imploding than it was twenty-five years ago. As Mr. Greenspan explains later, an implosion of our monetary system can, in his word, be "thwarted" only by creating money, possibly without limit. Here is why.

As the capital markets have become more efficient, very credit-worthy borrowers have been bypassing banks and have gone directly to the capital markets. For example, when IBM or General Motors need funding, they sell securities into the commercial paper market. In this way, they pay a lower interest rate than if they borrowed from banks.

Banks, in turn, in order to continue to profit by generating interest and fees from *creating* deposits, i.e., money, by extending credit, have had to lend to less credit-worthy borrowers and for less liquid investments, such as real estate. Thus, the quality of bank assets (their loan and investment book) has decreased. This has increased the probability that there will be a default by marginal borrowers and the concomitant probability that banks will have to access the Fed's Discount Window, i.e., cause the Federal Reserve to act as the "lender of last resort."

In the event that the Federal Reserve is called upon to bail out banks and other financial institutions, the amount of money that may be created to do so has no limit. Therefore, as banks continue to create money by extending credit to less credit-worthy borrowers, the "unconstrained issuance of claims" becomes less "remote." This is a very unstable situation.

Parenthetically, this predicament is not limited to the U.S. All around the world, in Japan, Korea, Indonesia, and elsewhere, banks—and monetary systems—are in trouble. In those cases, it is the rich who are being bailed out. Meanwhile, ordinary working people are being crushed by the system.

Second, according to Mr. Peter Peterson, writing in the *Atlantic Monthly*, the U.S. Government fiscal deficit on an *accrual* basis is $1.5 *trillion* per year. Concerning the so-called privatization of Social Security, I am told that Dr. Milton Friedman estimates that, to issue bonds to those presently entitled to receive benefits, the government would have to book another $8 *trillion* in liabilities in addition to that which has already been booked.

If one assigns any reasonable interest rate to what would then be the National Debt, then Mr. Peterson's estimate is justified. This large amount (now approaching $20 trillion) cannot be made up by taxes.[12]

Either: (a) promises of anticipated benefits will be broken (changed); (b) large amounts of additional money will be created; or, (c) a combination of the two.[13]

Thus, the chances of creating money to meet these obligations are also not "remote." The amount of money created will depend upon the mood of the country and who is in office. My guess is that seniors will not vote for politicians who decrease their benefits, and who can blame them?

Mr. Greenspan enlightens us:

> "The law of supply and demand is not to be conned. As the supply of money (of claims) increases relative to the supply of tangible assets in the economy, prices must eventually rise. Thus, the earnings saved by the productive members of the society lose value in terms of goods. When the economy's books

15

are finally balanced, one finds that this loss in value represents the goods purchased by the government for welfare or other purposes with the money proceeds of the government bonds financed by bank credit expansion."[14]

Mr. Greenspan's reference to interest rates being higher because of inflationary "expectations" is right on the mark. Very importantly, interest rates would be much lower if we resumed gold-as-money. There is more than two hundred years' of empirical evidence to support this view. For example, a chart of long-term interest rates in the United Kingdom from 1731 to 1970 shows that:

"The briefest glance at this chart of 240 years of English interest rates shows . . . for more than 200 years, England maintained stable long-term interest rates through a rigid gold standard. Long-term rates never got above 6 percent and never fell below 3 percent, and in most years wiggled hardly a jiggle. And England suffered little of the inflation that periodically racked other countries. And they did all this throughout the course of famines, pestilence, numerous major wars (Napoleonic Wars, World Wars I and II, etc.) and the greatest upheaval of modern times, the Industrial Revolution."[15]

More importantly, there is a proxy for gold-based debt that trades on the New York Stock Exchange. It is the Freeport-McMoRan Preferred Stock. It pays a dividend based on the price of gold and it is redeemable in the year 2003 also based on the price of gold. Because lenders are protected by gold, the Freeport-McMoRan Company, a B-rated company, was in 1993 able to borrow ten-year money at less than 4 percent while the United States Government, presumably an entity with a better credit rating, was then paying nearly 7 percent interest for the same ten-year money.

Issues that ought to be raised, especially by those who represent ordinary working people, i.e., Organized Labor, are:

Mindful of how important low interest rates are for creating jobs, why shouldn't we have the monetary system that guarantees the lowest possible interest rate?

Why should working peoples' jobs be sacrificed to higher interest rates so that banks can continue to benefit from their monopoly on fiat money creation?

Pressures for increased credit unrelated to the needs of markets emerge not only as a consequence of new government debt obligations, both direct and contingent, but also because of government regulations that *induce* private sector expenditure and borrowing. [Emphasis added.]

For example, Government-guaranteed debt obligations for Government Sponsored Entities, such as Fannie Mae, are now more than $7 trillion. It is not credible to conclude that the government will never be called upon to make good on some of these guarantees. This is a contingent liability that is not included in the Federal Budget; it is a non-cash item. In addition to these are promises that politicians have made to seniors, e.g.,

Social Security and Medicaid benefits, which represent an unstated liability of nearly $10 trillion.

The key word here is "induce." Were the government not to guarantee these obligations, then they would have to stand or fall on their own merits, and there would be fewer of them.

All of these government-derived demands on resources must be satisfied. Hence, when those demands increase, interest rates rise and crowd out other types of spending.

The "other types of spending" that are being "crowded out" include investments in productive facilities that would create jobs and improve our standard of living.[16] The reason they are crowded out is that since the government can always cause the banking system to monetize its debt, it can never default. Accordingly, it has the best credit rating and its debt gets serviced before all others no matter how high the interest rate.

Any employment of the sovereign credit rating for the issuance of government debt, the guaranteeing of the liabilities of depository institutions [such as banks], or the liquification of assets ["liquification" means exchanging assets which cannot be sold, such as assets that may be worthless, for the Fed's newly-created money] of depository institutions enables the preemption of real private resources by government fiat.

Increased availability of a central bank credit facility, even if not drawn upon, can *induce increased credit extension by banks and increased activity by their customers, since creditors of banks are more willing to finance banks' activities with such a governmental backstop available.* [Emphasis added.]

The "preemption of real private resources by government fiat" is actually wealth transfer from those whose resources are preempted, such as the purchasing power of the accumulated savings and pensions of ordinary working people and seniors, to "depository institutions" such as banks. When Mr. Greenspan says that "increased availability of a central bank credit facility . . . can induce . . . increased activity by their [banks'] customers," he is saying that they can increase leverage too. There is a pyramid effect.

In other words, since depositors know that the Federal Reserve will bail out banks if banks become insolvent, depositors become indifferent about putting their money in (lending to) banks regardless of the risks banks take. At the same time, banks are "induced" to leverage more and take greater risks since they also know that the Federal Reserve will rescue them if need be. As a result, despite the enormous risks that banks take, they are able to pay less interest to depositors. This deprives savers of interest to which they are entitled, and, at the same time, enables banks to make riskier bets and amass bigger profits.

If that takes place in an environment of strained resource availability, *expanded subsidies to depository institutions—which are often referred to as the "safety net"*—can only augment the pressures. [Emphasis added.]

Mr. Greenspan is making an important point: he is saying that the "safety net" that taxpayers provide to banks really constitutes a subsidy. By definition, a subsidy entails wealth transfer. In this case, ordinary taxpayers are transferring wealth to banks. For the remainder of this speech, every time Mr. Greenspan says "safety net," think "subsidy/wealth transfer."

The Federal Reserve Bank of Minneapolis enlightens us further:

"The subsidy the bankers receive from deposit insurance has two components, each of which has tangible value. First, the insurance reduces the cost of bank liabilities [deposits which banks take in]. Banks have access to funds at rates lower than those paid by uninsured financial institutions. Moreover, it is clear from the worst period of the bank failures of the 1980s that even the most conspicuously unsound banks have access to deposits at rates only marginally greater than rates offered by sound banks. The second component of the deposit insurance subsidy is lower capital than would otherwise be required by the marketplace. A lower capital requirement means a bank has the opportunity to be more leveraged and take on more risk. Even those who will hold that a stable banking system requires a policy of 'too-big-to-fail,' acknowledge that bank capital has declined dramatically since the institution of deposit insurance."[17]

Questions:

How much money is being transferred from workers and other ordinary taxpayers to the banks by virtue of these subsidies?

Why in a democracy should we permit a monetary system that causes poorer people (ordinary taxpayers) to transfer wealth to richer people (bankers)?

An accommodative monetary policy can ease the strain, but only temporarily and only at the risk of inflation at a later date *unless interest rates are eventually allowed to rise.* [Emphasis added.]

This is so pivotal, I want to rephrase it. Because banks know that they can rely on the Federal Reserve as a lender of last resort to bail them out if they experience catastrophic losses from bad loans, bad derivative bets, trading losses or other bad "investments," banks are "induced" to take on more risk. But, to constrain bank risk taking, interest rates must be "allowed to rise," thereby snuffing out jobs. Why ordinary working people put up with this kind of monetary system is a mystery to me.

Let me put this still another way. An accommodative monetary policy means manipulating interest rates lower usually by creating money out of nothing, a process called Federal Open Market Operations.[18] Mr. Greenspan points out that this risks inflation. Actually, the creation of any amount of money out of nothing is stealing and is inflationary.

If an increase in the rate of inflation is anticipated, the market adds an "inflation premium" to interest rates, marginal borrowers begin to default and, unless the Federal Reserve acts promptly by supplying "liquidity," the threat of a deflationary spiral increases. On the other hand, supplying "liquidity" is highly inflationary.

This is an element of systemic risk which Mr. Greenspan would like to dampen. Better the Federal Reserve should increase interest rates to constrain bank leverage before the market does so on its own. Thus, "interest rates are eventually allowed to rise," thereby snuffing out jobs. Either way, ordinary working people and seniors are losers. The winners are banks and Wall Street firms.

Question:

Is it fair to ordinary working people and seniors that the Federal Reserve "allows interest rates to rise" in order to constrain systemic risk and future inflation which is intensified by a subsidy that ordinary taxpayers are forced by Law to provide to the banks?[19]

Parenthetically, the Federal Reserve targets wage increases, especially in the service sector as a "cause" of inflation. This is another way in which ordinary working people suffer so that banks can profit from money creation. A recent Federal Reserve Bank of New York study confirms this.

> "The results presented here confirm a link from service sector wages and prices to overall inflation. We find that if compensation growth accelerates in the service-producing sector, that growth is likely to show up directly as more rapid inflation in service prices. Moreover, higher hourly labor costs in services can, through their contribution to the production and distribution of goods, indirectly affect goods prices. Given earlier researchers' findings showing a link from prices to wages, even these

modest initial effects may therefore be enough to set off an inflationary spiral. Since no such effects are found to arise from an acceleration of the labor cost increases in the goods-producing sector, policymakers seeking to prevent a resurgence of inflation may wish to pay particular attention to hourly labor costs in the service-producing private sector."[20,21]

This dilemma is most historically evident in its extreme form during times of war, when governments must choose whether to finance part of the increased war outlays through increased central bank credit [money creation] or depend wholly on taxes and borrowing from private sources.

Mr. Greenspan has omitted an important issue. The Federal Reserve is not the only entity that creates money to purchase government bonds (called "monetizing the debt"). Banks have monetized almost twice the amount of government debt than has the Fed. But, whereas the Federal Reserve returns to the Treasury interest that it receives from government bonds purchased with money that it creates (less the Fed's expenses), banks *keep for their own account* interest on bonds that they bought with money that they created. As of this writing, the banks' U.S. Government bond portfolio totals nearly $900 billion.[22]

Questions:

Why should banks be allowed to keep "interest"—now nearly $50 billion *per year*—paid by our government (and collected from ordinary taxpayers) on bonds which they bought with money that they created simply by keying numbers into a computer terminal? That is, they didn't have to do any work and save to acquire the bonds, as other citizens must. Why should they get $50 billion per year in interest virtually for doing nothing?[23]

Isn't this another example of wealth transfer from ordinary taxpayers to bankers; from poorer people to richer people?

Accordingly central banks, and finance ministries, must remain especially vigilant in maintaining a proper balance between a safety net [subsidy/wealth transfer] that fosters economic and financial stabilization and one that does not. It is in this context of competing demands for resources and the government's unique position that we should consider the role of the central bank in interfacing with [regulating] banks, and in some instances with other private financial institutions [e.g., Wall Street firms and insurance companies], as lenders of last resort, supervisors, and providers of financial services.

In other words, since taxpayers are subsidizing—transferring wealth to—banks and, to some extent, Wall Street firms, the Federal Reserve must regulate them to prevent excesses that would inevitably occur under such an arrangement. Another way of saying this is that because taxpayers are subsidizing banks and Wall Street firms, and because the amount of the subsidy is potentially limitless, the Federal Reserve must regulate them to prevent them from exploiting the safety net/subsidy in the extreme.

Question:

What evidence is there that banks and Wall Street firms are not *already* exploiting the safety net/subsidy in the extreme?

Mr. Greenspan takes it as a given that the safety net/subsidy/wealth transfer that favors the financial sector is something that ought to exist in a democracy, when it ought not.

Relationship to banks and bank supervision

It is important to remember that many of the benefits banks provide modern societies derive from their willingness to take risks and from their use of a relatively high degree of financial leverage. Through leverage, in the form principally of taking deposits, banks perform a critical role in the financial intermediation process; they provide savers **[mostly working people seeking safety]** with additional investment choices and borrowers **[mostly large and credit-worthy—when working people borrow from banks, for example on their credit cards, they pay exorbitant interest and punitive fees]** with a greater range of sources of credit, thereby facilitating a more efficient allocation of resources and contributing importantly to greater economic growth.[24]

The concept of a "bank deposit" is a material misrepresentation with roots going back to the 17th century. It has been responsible for much suffering. A "deposit" in a bank is in fact and in law a loan to the bank. The money "deposited" becomes the bank's money and it goes on the bank's balance sheet as a liability.

Courts have ruled that banks may do with the money as they wish, e.g., they may lend the money, they may make derivative bets, or they may invest the money in almost anything including real estate or stocks.[25] Thus, a "depositor" is in fact and in law an unsecured lender to the bank. Most people don't understand this. They think that money "deposited" in a bank remains *their* money. The banks encourage this misperception by assuring people that they may withdraw "their" money "on demand."

Mr. Greenspan's interpretation is not supported by the facts. The banking system does *not* facilitate more efficient allocation of resources and it does *not* contribute to "greater economic growth." Because of its monopoly on money creation and because of the safety net/subsidy, it mostly facilitates wealth transfer from working people and from seniors to banks, to Wall Street firms, and to large credit-worthy borrowers. Here is a partial explanation.

With minor exception, banks have increased leverage by mismatching their liabilities, i.e., money which they owe depositors who are in fact lenders to banks, and their assets, i.e., money which banks lend to others or which banks invest. Most important, banks don't merely lend money that has been deposited. Banks *create* deposits.[26]

For example, when a bank extends a loan to someone for $100,000, it does so by crediting that person's account in that amount. After the loan has been granted, not one depositor has any less money on deposit than before the loan was granted. If all depositors' balances are unchanged, from where does the $100,000 come?

It is "created" by the bank as the result of a mere bookkeeping entry. Bankers garner fees and interest for extending loans by means of this newly-created money.[27] Since 1947, banks in the U.S. have created more than $7 trillion.

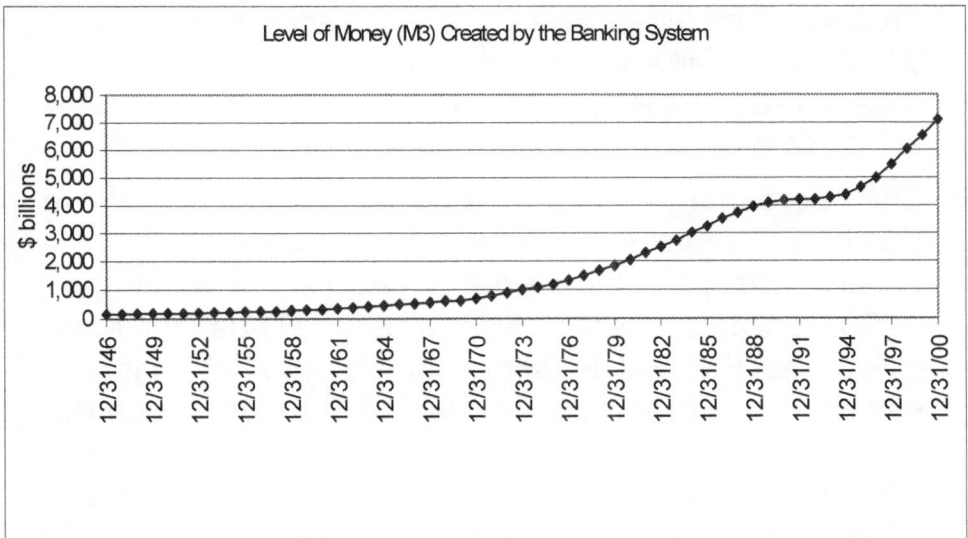

Figure 1: *Level of Money (M3) Created by the banking system* (Source: Federal Reserve *H.6 Series* for the period 1959 to present; and the *Historical Statistics of the United States: Colonial Times to 1970*; Series X-415, X-418, X-419; U.S. Department of Commerce for the period 1946-1958.)

Banks usually have arrangements with depositors whereby depositors may retrieve their money *on demand*. However, money committed by banks to borrowers and to investments is *not* retrievable on demand. In other words, banks are mismatching their assets and their liabilities.[28] This is a problem. It is camouflaged by the fact that most of the money lent to borrowers is either left in the bank that originally lent it or redeposited into another bank.

Banks increase leverage by relending the same money (less a small portion kept in "reserve"), by investing it, and by making bets in the financial markets (called "trading"). Economists say this contributes to "economic growth." But, this so-called "growth" is merely leveraging of the same assets, each additional round of which yields fees and interest to banks and transaction fees to Wall Street firms. Moreover, it puts the economy at risk to a gigantic bust.

The percentage banks keep in reserve in case someone wants to withdraw their money is the so-called "Reserve Requirement." As recent as August 1993, It was a mere 1.65 percent.[29] Thus, for each dollar the Federal Reserve injects into the banking system, banks may create ("lend") $60. One need not be a rocket scientist to realize that this is inflationary. The banks do it because they get a multiple on the interest and fees they would receive if they merely performed intermediation, i.e., accumulated deposits and loaned them within the same time frames.

Indeed, it has been the evident value of intermediation and leverage that has shaped the development of our financial systems from the earliest times—certainly since Renaissance goldsmiths discovered that lending out deposited gold was feasible and profitable.

Some gain from this "intermediation and leverage," which is synonymous with money creation, and some lose. The winners are banks, Wall Street firms, and large credit-worthy borrowers. They wouldn't go along with this arrangement if this were not so. The losers are ordinary working people, savers and other taxpayers. They go along with it because relevant information is misrepresented and not disclosed. It does not have "evident value" as Mr. Greenspan suggests, unless you are a bank, a Wall Street firm, or a large credit-worthy borrower.

It is true that goldsmiths lent out deposited gold, but this was dishonest. Because the gold had been left with them for safekeeping, and was not to be put at risk, goldsmiths were in fact guilty of the crime of conversion. They were using for their own ends gold which they had a fiduciary responsibility to keep safe.[30]

The fact that the gold may have been returned to depositors is beside the point. The goldsmiths were putting depositors at risk without their permission, without making proper disclosure, and without compensating them for that risk. Goldsmiths kept that compensation—the interest—for themselves. In effect, the goldsmiths were misappropriating interest on money that was left with them for safekeeping.

Thus, when Mr. Greenspan says that "lending out deposited gold was feasible and profitable," he means that it was feasible and profitable for the goldsmiths and the (presumably) credit-worthy borrowers to whom they lent the gold. In time, banks increased leverage by lending gold certificates that were not fully backed by gold, i.e., they engaged in fractional reserve lending. FAME Foundation scholar Edwin Vieira explains the essence of fractional reserve lending:

"Under fractional-reserve banking, the bank always issues more units of fiduciary money, supposedly 'payable on demand', than it has units of commodity money available for redemption, counting on the unlikelihood that the majority of its customers will ever seek redemption at one time. Thus, modern fractional reserve banking is inherently fraudulent, because:

1. For the bank simultaneously to fulfill all its promises to redeem its outstanding notes 'on demand' is impossible.

2. The bank's managers know that complete redemption 'on demand' is impossible, and therefore that the bank's promises to pay are false. And,

3. The bank's customers, by and large, are ignorant of how the fractional-reserve scheme works, and the dangers it poses to them."[31]

When the banking system developed, and banks issued what were really warehouse receipts for gold deposits, the courts consistently allowed banks to lend out depositors' money. Courts took the position that the promise of repayment was a civil matter. As economist Dr. Mark Skousen explains:

"During the 17th and 18th centuries, bank customers filed suit over fractional reserve banking and the legal status of customers' deposits. In nearly every case, the courts ruled consistently that the banker was only a debtor and not a bailee or trustee. Why? Principally because the money or coins in storage were not specifically identifiable. This was the *sine qua non* in any case involving theft or robbery of property — the stolen property or goods must, according to the courts, be identifiable. . . . the only action for the recovery of money is one of debt."[32]

It was noted, however, that the term "deposit" was misleading.[33] Fractional reserve lending can thus be seen as a form of leveraging. As with all leveraging, gains and losses are magnified by the leverage factor. The Federal Reserve was created to be a lender of last resort to mute deleveraging in the event of defaults on money owed to banks. As Mr. Greenspan repeatedly explains, just the existence of the Federal Reserve enables banks to engage in more leverage than otherwise. The consequence of this for ordinary people has historically been disastrous.

For example, in the 1930's, when depositors realized that banks lost money lent to stock speculators, and for illiquid investments such as real estate, depositors attempted to withdraw their money, as they were entitled to do, "just in case." Some banks had lost significant money and were insolvent. Others, which might have survived except for the many withdrawals, had to deleverage, i.e., sell assets (loans) and not renew loans when they came due (known as "calling a loan").[34] Many depositors were so distrustful of the financial system, they attempted to exchange their money for gold, as they were also entitled to do.

However, because the Federal Reserve had, using Mr. Greenspan's word, "induced" banks to create so much extra credit (dollars)—all of which were theoretically "payable to the bearer on demand in gold," there wasn't enough gold in the Treasury to redeem the Federal Reserve Notes. It was for this reason that President Roosevelt seized the nation's gold and unilaterally erased the Gold Clause from all existing contracts. Here is President Roosevelt's confusing and disingenuous explanation:

> "Much has been said of late about Federal finances and inflation, the gold standard, etc. Let me make the facts very simple and my policy very clear. In the first place, government credit and government currency are really one and the same thing. Behind government bonds there is only a promise to pay. Behind government currency we have, in addition to the promise to pay, a reserve of gold and a small reserve of silver."

> "In this connection it is worthwhile remembering that in the past the government has agreed to redeem nearly thirty billions of its debts and its currency in gold, and private corporations in this country have agreed to redeem another sixty or seventy billions of securities and mortgages in gold. The government and private corporations were making these agreements when they knew full well that all of the gold in the United States amounted to only between three and four billions and that all of the gold in all of the world amounted to only about eleven billions."

"If the holders of these promises to pay started in to demand gold the first comers would get gold for a few days and they would amount to about one twenty-fifth of the holders of the securities and the currency. The other twenty-four people out of twenty-five, who did not happen to be at the top of the line, would be told politely that there was no more gold left. We have decided to treat all twenty-five in the same way in the interest of justice and the exercise of the constitutional powers of this government. We have placed every one on the same basis in order that the general good may be preserved."[35]

"What, then, happened during the last few days of February and the first few days of March? Because of undermined confidence on the part of the public, there was a general portion of our population to turn bank deposits into currency or gold. — A rush so great that the soundest banks could not get enough currency to meet the demand. The reason for this was that on the spur of the moment it was, of course, impossible to sell perfectly sound assets of a bank and convert them into cash except at panic prices far below their real value."[36]

Thus, this *prima facie* unconstitutional—but not adjudicated unconstitutional—arrangement, whereby the taxpayers are obligated by Law to subsidize banks, caused incalculable suffering.

A good case can be made that the Federal Reserve under Mr. Greenspan has committed the same errors in the 1990's as did the Federal Reserve in the 1920's and that there is great risk of a complete meltdown of our financial system. Mr. Greenspan alludes to this later in this speech.[37]

Central bank provision of a mechanism for converting highly illiquid portfolios [portfolios that cannot be sold] into liquid ones [into cash] in extraordinary circumstances has led to a greater degree of leverage in banking than market forces alone would support. [Private investors would pay less for these assets than would the Fed. In fact, depending upon how "illiquid" these portfolios are, private investors might pay nothing.]

Mr. Greenspan is confirming that the "mechanism" or safety net/subsidy/wealth transfer for banks, has led to more leverage than would otherwise occur. For banks, this is great. They can enter into more profitable and riskier bets than they would otherwise because they know that if they lose, i.e., if their bets become "illiquid"—worthless and cannot be sold—the Federal Reserve will "convert" those bets into cash.

And where does the Federal Reserve get the cash? It literally "creates" it out of nothing, thereby diluting the purchasing power of savings and expected pensions of ordinary working people and seniors. In other words, if the banks win their bets they keep their winnings, and if they lose, the Fed—read that ordinary taxpayers—absorb the losses. Fantastic!

Traditionally this has been accomplished by making discount or Lombard facilities available, so that individual depositories could turn illiquid assets [assets that cannot be sold at par, or perhaps not sold at all] into liquid resources [cash] and not

34

exacerbate unsettled market conditions by the forced selling of such assets or the calling of loans.

What this means is that rather than cause "individual depositories" (banks) to sell "illiquid assets" (loans) which are not good—at a presumed loss—or force borrowers into bankruptcy, the Federal Reserve may buy these loans from the banks, presumably at a discount. Again, if things work out, the banks keep the profits. If the loans cannot be repaid, the Federal Reserve (really taxpayers) makes up the loss.

Question:

Is it fair to taxpayers that banks keep the winnings if their bets are successful but that taxpayers make them good if they experience catastrophic losses? Isn't this just blatant wealth transfer?[38]

More broadly, open market operations, in situations like that which followed the crash of stock markets around the world in 1987, satisfy increased needs for liquidity for the system as a whole that otherwise could feed cumulative, self-reinforcing, contractions across many financial markets.

In this and other speeches, Mr. Greenspan addresses systemic risk. Much more needs to be said about this, but, in sum, the system is perilously close to imploding or blowing up.

Question:

Why should ordinary citizens be at risk that our monetary system will implode so that banks and other financial players may reap unearned profits by taking on ever-greater risks?

Of course, this same leverage and risk-taking also greatly increase the possibility of bank failures. Without leverage, losses from risk-taking would be absorbed by a bank's owners, virtually eliminating the chance that the bank would be unable to meet its obligations in the case of a "failure."

In other words, without the safety net/subsidy from taxpayers, banks would make bets and take chances while putting their <u>own</u> capital at risk instead of taxpayers' money. This is as it should be, it seems to me. Most important, Mr. Greenspan confirms that without leverage the possibility that depositors would not get their money back in case of a "failure" would be *virtually eliminated*. Ordinary working people and seniors would not be at risk.

What an incredible acknowledgment! In other words, we can conclude that if the banks had not been induced by the safety net/subsidy to increase leverage, the banking system would not have collapsed in the 1930's and we would not have experienced the Great Depression. Many think that the Great Depression was a "market failure." Mr. Greenspan has written extremely eloquently that the Great Depression was in fact caused by the Federal Reserve feeding too much credit into the banking system, i.e., enabling the banking system to increase leverage too much.[39]

This raises other important questions:

Why should our government empower and induce banks to increase leverage when we know that can lead, and has led, to a catastrophic monetary collapse? Why should ordinary working people and seniors and

the rest of us be put at risk of a monetary implosion and the total collapse of our economy?

Some failures can be of a bank's own making, resulting, for example, from poor credit judgments. For the most part, these failures are a normal and important part of the market process and provide discipline and information to other participants regarding the level of business risks. However, because of the important roles that banks and other financial intermediaries **[Who does he have in mind? Wall Street firms?]** play in our financial systems, such failures could have large ripple effects that spread throughout business and financial markets at great cost.

But he has already told us that this "great cost" could be "virtually eliminated" if banks were not subsidized and induced to increase leverage. Further, it is only because of the safety net/subsidy, along with misrepresenting to depositors that they may always retrieve their money "on demand" that banks are able to increase leverage in the first place.

Question:

Again, why in a democracy are we willing to risk our economic lives so that one group of private companies—banks—can increase leverage and reap massive unearned profits?

Any use of sovereign credit—even its potential use—creates moral hazard, that is, a distortion of incentives that occurs when the party that determines the level of risk **[e.g., banks and Wall Street firms]** receives the gains from, but does not bear the full costs of, the risks taken. **[This is really straight talk: The financial sector keeps its winnings, but if it loses someone else pays. It's like heads the financial sector wins; tails the taxpayers lose.]**

At the extreme, monetary authorities could guarantee all private liabilities, which might assuage any immediate crisis but leave a long-term legacy of distorted incentives and presumably thwarted growth potential. Thus, governments, including central banks, have to strive for a balanced use of the sovereign credit rating. It is a difficult tradeoff, but we are seeking a balance *in which we can ensure the desired degree of intermediation* [emphasis added] even in times of financial stress without engendering an unacceptable degree of moral hazard.

Questions:

Why should politicians be in charge of determining how much risk banks may take and then subsidizing those risks with taxpayer money? (Remember, these are the same politicians that received $2.4 *billion* in campaign "contributions" at the national level only in the 1996 general election.)

None of this was explicitly authorized by our elected representatives or by our *Constitution!* In other words, it is not lawful!

How come those who want the *Constitution* to be interpreted the way it was written and not the way judges wish it were written don't object to this injustice?[40]

The disconnect between risk-taking by banks and banks' cost of capital, *which has been reduced by the presence of the safety net*, has made necessary a degree of supervision and regulation that would not be necessary without the existence of the safety net [subsidy]. [Emphasis added.]

Here, Mr. Greenspan confirms yet again that the safety net is also a subsidy to banks and a cost to savers and taxpayers because it enables banks to operate with

less capital and to pay lower interest rates than they would otherwise.

That is, regulators are compelled to act as a surrogate for market discipline since the *market signals that usually accompany excessive risk-taking are substantially muted* **[emphasis added]**, and because the prices to banks of government deposit guarantees, or of access to the safety net **[subsidy]** more generally, do not, and probably cannot, vary sufficiently with risk to mimic market prices.

He is saying that if the banks were not regulated, they might milk the safety net/subsidy to the extreme.

Question:

For the second time, what evidence is there that banks are not *already* exploiting the safety net/subsidy to the extreme despite Mr. Greenspan's efforts at regulation?

The problems that arise from the retarding of the pressures of market discipline have led us increasingly to understand that the ideal strategy for supervision and regulation is to endeavor to simulate the market responses that would occur if there were no safety net **[subsidy]**, but without giving up the basic requirement that financial market disruptions be minimized.

Thus, the Federal Reserve regulates the financial sector as a substitute for market forces. But, we know from the experience of the Soviet Empire that bureaucratic tinkering with the economy doesn't work.

Questions:

Why should the Fed, a central planner *par excellence*, succeed where all other central planners have failed?

What makes Mr. Greenspan, or anyone else, think that he can outguess the market?

Also, and more importantly, why attempt to "simulate market responses?"

Why shouldn't banks and Wall Street firms play by the same rules as the rest of us? Who made them a special class of citizen to be subsidized by taxpayers?

Why should their unfair quest for unearned profits be allowed to put the rest of us at risk to a catastrophic meltdown of our financial system and our economy?

To be sure, we should recognize that if we choose to have the *advantages of a leveraged* [emphasis added] ["Advantages" to whom? Certainly not to ordinary working people who have to cope with higher interest rates, and certainly not to seniors who have seen their savings and pensions eroded by inflation!] system of financial intermediaries, the burden of managing risk in the financial system will not lie with the private sector alone.

If the "burden" (the cost) does not lie with the private sector, then it lies with the public sector, with taxpayers. This means that wealth is being transferred from taxpayers to a particular group of citizens: those who have a stake in financial firms.

With leveraging there will always exist a *remote* [emphasis added] possibility of a chain reaction, a cascading sequence of defaults that will culminate in financial implosion if it proceeds unchecked.

Questions:

Again, why should we have a monetary system that puts us at risk of a financial implosion?

Our system of government, as defined by our *Constitution*, protects us from this risk by providing that only gold and silver be money.[41] Neither our elected representatives nor we ever explicitly voted to change that.

More to the point, why shouldn't we have the gold standard system that Mr. Greenspan implies would "virtually eliminate" the possibility of catastrophic failure?

Also, how "remote" is "the possibility of a chain reaction, a cascading sequence of defaults that will culminate in financial implosion if it proceeds unchecked?"

In his speech at the International Conference of Banking Supervisors, Stockholm, Sweden on June 13, 1996, Mr. Greenspan spoke of the taxpayer being potentially asked to bear "some of the cost of [systemic] failure." He said: "Activating such risk sharing quite appropriately occurs at most two to three times a century." *Two or three times a century!* This should not be acceptable to ordinary working people and seniors or anyone else.

Only a central bank, with its unlimited power to create money [*There!* He finally said it straight, and for the *fifth* time in this speech. No more talk about "creating claims" or "converting illiquid assets into liquid ones!" Just the "unlimited power" to create money out of nothing! This was not agreed to by voters, nor by our elected representatives, nor authorized by our *Constitution*.], can with a high probability [But not a certainty! And that's why we're all at unacceptable and unwarranted risk! While we're at it, how high is "high"?] thwart such a process [by bailing out the banks at taxpayer expense] before it becomes destructive.

Hence, central banks will of necessity be drawn into becoming lenders of last resort. [It is crucial to understand that such "lending" by the central bank involves money creation and is just another way of transferring wealth from savers and ordinary working people, who are due pensions payable in dollars, to banks.] But implicit in the existence of such a role is that there will be some sort of allocation between the public and private sectors of the burden of risk of extreme outcomes. Thus, central banks are led to provide what essentially amounts to catastrophic financial insurance coverage.

This is a complete misstatement. In no way can the role of central banks be properly characterized as providing "insurance." Because of the inherent "moral hazard," there is no insurable risk. As Professor Murray Rothbard has written:

> "Insurance is only an appropriate term and a feasible concept when there are certain near-measurable risks that can be pooled over large numbers of cases: fire, accident, disease, etc. But an entrepreneurial firm or industry cannot be 'insured,' since the entrepreneur is undertaking the sort of risks that precisely cannot be measured or pooled, and hence cannot be insured against."[42]

Such a *public subsidy* [emphasis added] [A "public subsidy" is just another way of saying "wealth transfer"] should be reserved for only the rarest of disasters. [In his June 13, 1996 speech in Stockholm, Mr. Greenspan said that these disasters occur "two or three times a century."]

Questions:

How "rare" is two or three times a century? And, what is the justification for this estimate?

How do we know such failures won't become more frequent?

Mindful that a "public subsidy" is really wealth transfer from ordinary taxpayers to the financial sector, is there any limit on how much wealth may be transferred? Or, as Mr. Greenspan puts it, is the amount *"without limit?"*

If the owners or managers of private financial institutions were to anticipate being propped up frequently by government support, it would only encourage reckless and irresponsible practices.

Question:

How reckless and irresponsible do banking practices need become before Mr. Greenspan considers them so?

Today, the banking system has made more than $60 *trillion* worth of derivative bets.[43] When I was growing up, these numbers were reserved for astronomy.

43

Questions:

Is $60 trillion in derivative bets "reckless and irresponsible?"

Will it be "reckless and irresponsible" when the amount of bets reaches $100 trillion?

How is "reckless and irresponsible" determined?

Do taxpayers, who will be called upon to make good if these bets fail (but who do not share in the winnings), have oversight through their elected representatives in the Congress, or is all of this left to Mr. Greenspan's discretion?

Perhaps Mr. Greenspan will one day share with us his criteria for "reckless and irresponsible practices."

In theory, the allocation of responsibility for risk-bearing between the private sector and the central bank depends upon an evaluation of the private cost of capital. In order to attract, or at least retain, capital, a private financial institution must earn at minimum the overall economy's rate of return, adjusted for risk. In competitive financial markets, the greater the leverage, the higher the rate of return, before adjustment for risk. *If private financial institutions have to absorb all financial risk, then the degree to which they can leverage will be limited, the financial sector smaller, and its contribution to the economy more limited.* [Emphasis added]

In other words, financial institutions, e.g., banks and Wall Street firms, wouldn't leverage as much if their own money were at risk. They would be smaller firms, and their "contribution to the economy," whatever that may be, would be less. Please be mindful that "their contribution to the economy" is in this case really a subsidy paid for by workers, seniors, and other taxpayers.

Moreover, this so-called "contribution to the economy" is misleading. What is really happening is wealth transfer from workers and seniors to banks and Wall Street firms. To the extent that their operations are counted in the "economy," of course there is a "contribution." However, it is an unearned contribution resulting from money created out of nothing.

This is a well-known phenomenon.

> "Protecting banks against runs destroys the incentive to maintain capital and leads to a substitution of public capital, reflected in the deposit insurance guarantee (or, for that matter, a lender of last resort policy), for the equity capital they would otherwise have maintained. . . A bank's rational response to deposit insurance is therefore to drive its capital ratio right down, and a weaker capital position leaves it more exposed to losses that could wipe out its net worth and drive it into economic insolvency."[44]

Question:

Why do people put up with this? Is it because they don't understand it? Or is it because there have been significant misrepresentations and nondisclosure.

On the other hand, if central banks effectively insulate private institutions from the largest potential losses, however incurred, increased laxity could *threaten a major drain on taxpayers or produce inflationary instability as a consequence of excess money creation.* [Emphasis added.]

<u>There</u>! Mr. Greenspan has again used plain language to describe the harmful consequence of providing a safety net to financial institutions. The cost of the safety net for banks is a potential "major drain on taxpayers"—read that ordinary working people and seniors—or a huge creation of new money out of nothing—really inappropriately transferring wealth from savers—leading to "inflationary instability."

Think of it as stealing from the poor to give to the rich. In essence, this is why our fiat money system is doomed to failure. Either we make an orderly transition to an honest system, or we will face a discontinuity later.

A big risk with a discontinuity is that people may be so disillusioned with government, they change its form. It is unlikely, in my view, that they will opt for a freer society. This is the foundation on which tyrannies are built! As the Honorable Howard Buffett (Warren Buffett's father) wrote in 1948 when he was a U.S. Congressman from Nebraska:

> "Monetary chaos was followed in Germany by a Hitler; in Russia by all-out Bolshevism; and in other nations by more or less tyranny. It can take a nation to communism without external influences. Suppose the frugal savings of the humble people of America continue to deteriorate in the next 10 years as they have in the past 10 years? Some day the people will almost certainly flock to 'a man on horseback' who says he will stop inflation by price-fixing, wage-fixing, and rationing. When currency loses its exchange

value the processes of production and distribution are demoralized."[45]

When money melts, interest rates increase, the purchasing power of savings is wiped out and people lose their jobs—all through no fault of their own—government is discredited and most times people change their form of government. Also, I don't believe that our elected representatives are mindful that their careers are at risk. For example, as a result of the Great Depression, which in essence was a monetary failure, *laissez-faire* was permanently discredited. As noted author William Greider wrote:

"Classical economics taught that free markets would always seek and find a natural equilibrium, a self-correcting capacity that revived production and employment, once prices and wages fell low enough. In the Great Depression, the American economy did not revive. Neither did the rest of the world's. Year after year, as the social misery deepened and massive unemployment stretched on for more than a decade, the popular faith in free markets was shattered. . . The New Deal advanced a new creed: an activist national government must intervene to overcome the shortcomings and weaknesses of private enterprise. This new idea—government's obligation to manage the economy—was legitimized by the national trauma of Depression, embraced both in public opinion and in scholarly theory."[46]

Question:

When Mr. Greenspan posits a "major drain on taxpayers," how much could that be in absolute dollars? Is the total accumulated savings of all American workers too high?

In practice, the policy choice of how much, if any, of the extreme market risk that government authorities should absorb is fraught with many complexities.

Actually, it is unworkable. These "policy choices" are so complex that the outcome of even sound judgment is very uncertain.

Question:

When Mr. Greenspan says "if any," is he suggesting that it is not a proper function of government to absorb market risk for a particular group of private citizens?

Yet we central bankers make this decision every day, either explicitly or by default. *Moreover, we can never know for sure whether the decisions we made were appropriate.* [Emphasis added]

Here, Mr. Greenspan confirms that the Federal Reserve is gambling with our economic lives. Also, Mr. Greenspan knows that central planning doesn't work. As former Federal Reserve Board of Governor Larry Lindsey has said:

> "It's amazing when I go out in public that everyone thinks we know something that nobody else does. Given the amount of disagreement around this table, it's unclear that we know anything. But they all think we know something that nobody else does."[47]

Questions:

Again, why should the Federal Reserve have more success than other central planners?

Again, why should citizens be at risk that the Federal Reserve might not make "appropriate" decisions?

The question is not whether our actions are seen to have been necessary in retrospect; the absence of a fire does not mean that we should not have paid for fire insurance.

Questions:

Why should we live in a fire zone when we don't have to? Why allow ourselves to be put in harm's way so that the financial sector may be unjustly rewarded?

Why shouldn't we have a monetary system, such as the gold standard, for which the possibility of a complete collapse can be "virtually eliminated?"

Rather, the question is whether, ex ante, the probability of a systemic collapse was sufficient to warrant intervention.

Question:

Why is it now that Mr. Greenspan in almost all of his speeches mentions "systemic collapse," the possibility of a complete meltdown of our financial system?

Often, we cannot wait to see whether, in hindsight, the problem will be judged to have been an isolated event and largely benign. Thus, governments, including central banks, have been given certain responsibilities related to their banking and financial systems that must be balanced.

This misstates the case. The responsibilities that Mr. Greenspan speaks of were not just "given." There has been and continues to be substantial collusion between banks and politicians. Banks engage in extensive lobbying and other efforts to maintain and further their money-creation cartel and other special privileges.

In recent years, the amounts funneled by the financial sector to politicians have increased by an order of magnitude. Consider one small example:

> "Since last year, when the latest reform bill started moving through the House, the coffers of Democratic and Republican lawmakers and their national committees have been enriched by $7.4 million from securities firms, $6.8 million from insurers and $5.5 million from banks."[48]

All over the world, fiat money has been designated legal tender.

Questions:

If the fiat money is good money and would be preferred by the people, then why are Legal Tender Laws necessary?

Also, if the fiat money is not good and would not be preferred by the people, then why in a democracy should they be forced to accept it?

The result, according to the well-known Gresham's Law, is that good money, such as gold-as-money, has gone into hiding.

Another principal factor in the establishment of wealth transfer from ordinary taxpayers to banks is that the Federal Reserve has compromised the academic community. In 1994, Mr. Stephen Davies cited evidence collected by then Chairman of the House Banking Committee Henry Gonzalez showing that the Federal Reserve has spent millions hiring economic faculty members as "consultants." The article quotes Mr. Gonzalez:

> "The Federal Reserve employs hundreds of researchers in their research departments, but inexplicably also spends millions to pay hundreds of outside economic consultants. . . *The Federal Reserve is simply buying off potential critics by holding out contracts that offer academics extra money* and use of the Fed's facilities. No agency that has to justify its spending would dream of this kind of extravagance and waste." [Emphasis added.]

More telling, the article continues:

> "Moreover, the *Bond Buyer* has learned that in the case of the Federal Reserve Board, all contractors are required to sign a non-disclosure statement . . . broadly worded *to prohibit the release of any information relating to past, present or future activities that can be considered damaging to the Board.*"[49] (Emphasis added)

Intellectuals legitimatize ideas, and the banks have been buying off intellectuals for more than 90 years. As Professor Murray Rothbard wrote:

"The big bankers realized that one of the first steps in the march to a central bank was to win support of the nation's economists, academics, and financial experts. Fortunately for the reformers, two useful organizations for the mobilizations of academics were near at hand: the American Academy of Political and Social Science of Philadelphia, and the Academy of Political Science of Columbia University, both of which comprised leading corporate liberal businessmen, financiers, and corporate attorneys, as well as academics."

". . . During the same spring of 1910, the National Monetary Commission's numerous research volumes on various aspects of banking poured forth onto the market. The object was to swamp public opinion with a parade of impressive analytic and historical scholarship, all allegedly 'scientific' and 'value-free,' but all designed to further the agenda of a central bank."

". . . The then impressive sum of $50,000 was raised throughout the nation's banking and corporate community to finance the work of the Indianapolis Monetary Commission. New York City's large quota was raised by Morgan bankers Peabody and Orr, and a large contribution came from none other than J.P. Morgan himself."[50]

This campaign has been ongoing. Two groups that would have credibility with the public—the monetary wing of the economics profession and intellectuals—have been compromised. The result is that more than three generations of Americans have been "dumbed down" on the money issue.

It is important to recognize that historically the American people have always rejected fiat money. Gold and/or silver did not become money because some potentate or government designated it so. Gold (and silver) has been the choice of the people in open markets from antiquity.[51]

Furthermore, every time Americans have had the opportunity, they have always chosen gold- and/or silver-as-money:[52]

> 1 - At the time of the Revolution, Americans were repulsed by their experience with the fiat money of the day: continentals. There was even a derogatory saying "not worth a continental." As a result, the *Constitution* provided for gold- and/or silver-as-money;[53]
>
> 2 - When Andrew Jackson ran for President in 1832, he opposed paper money and the Bank of the United States. His rallying cry was "Gold is the friend of the farmer" [and the worker]—and Jackson won!;
>
> 3 - When President Grant signed the Resumption Legislation in 1874—doing away with the Civil War Greenbacks and resuming gold-as-money— he said he did it because it was "the right thing to do";[54] and,
>
> 4 - When McKinley (pro-gold) ran against Bryan (pro-silver/"Cross of Gold") in 1896, gold won again! Also, Bryan would never have tolerated fiat

money. He just wanted silver to participate as a monetary metal.

And, when President Roosevelt seized the gold in 1933, he reassured the country that our money would not be fiat.

> "Remember that the essential accomplishment of the new legislation is that it makes it possible for banks more readily to convert their assets into cash than was the case before. More liberal provision has been made for banks to borrow on these assets at the Reserve Banks and more liberal provision has also been made for issuing currency on the security of those good assets. *This currency is not fiat currency.* It is issued only on adequate security — and every good bank has an abundance of such security."[55] [Emphasis added.]

I think it is fair to conclude, therefore, that the monetary system we have now was not the choice of the people. Mr. Greenspan does us a disservice by glossing over this fact.

We have the responsibility to prevent major financial market disruptions through development and enforcement of prudent regulatory standards and, if necessary in rare circumstances, through direct intervention in market events.

Questions:

Is it reasonable to expect that "direct intervention in market events" includes intervention in the stock market? And if not, why not?

The Federal Reserve and other central banks already intervene in the fixed income and foreign exchange markets to maintain "stability." The Bank of Japan is known to intervene in the Japanese stock market. Why is it reasonable to think that the Federal Reserve does not—or would not—do this in the U.S.?

In the quest to maintain "stability," why should some markets be excluded?

Doesn't intervention in the fixed income markets and the currency markets mean that ordinary working people and seniors are also subsidizing (transferring wealth to) Wall Street firms?

Is that fair?

Did our elected representatives explicitly vote for this?

Does the *Constitution* empower government to do this?

Keep in mind that this intervention is for the benefit of banks and Wall Street firms—a special group of private companies who have been colluding with politicians.

But we also have the responsibility to ensure that private sector institutions have the capacity to take prudent and appropriate risks, even though such risks will sometimes result in unanticipated bank losses or even bank failures.

Questions:

From where did this "responsibility to ensure that private sector institutions to take prudent and appropriate risks" arise? Does Mr. Greenspan maintain that this is a responsibility that was decided upon by the voters or by their elected representatives?

Our goal as supervisors, therefore, should not be to prevent all bank failures, but to maintain sufficient prudential standards so that banking problems that do occur do not become widespread. We try to achieve the proper balance through official regulations, as well as through formal and informal supervisory policies and procedures.

To some extent, we do this over time by signaling to the market, through our actions **[primarily by manipulating the Federal Reserve Funds rate by injecting newly-created money into or taking money out of the banking system]**, the kinds of circumstances in which we might be willing to intervene to quell financial turmoil, and conversely, what levels of difficulties we expect private institutions to resolve by themselves. The market, then, responds by adjusting the cost of capital to banks.

In other words, interest rates increase. Also, the record of central banks is dismal. As former Federal Reserve Chairman Paul Volcker has stated:

> **"It is a sobering fact that the prominence of central banks in this century has coincided with a general tendency towards more inflation, not less. By and large, if the overriding objective is price stability, we did better with the nineteenth-century gold standard and passive central banks, with currency boards, or even with 'free banking'."[56]**

Throughout most of this century, we central bankers have made our decisions largely in a domestic context. However, in recent decades that situation has changed markedly for many countries and, obviously, is changing rapidly here in Europe.

While failures will inevitably occur in a dynamic market, the safety net **[subsidy]**—not to mention concerns over systemic risk **[the risk that the whole financial structure collapses despite the safety net/subsidy]**—requires that regulators not be indifferent to how banks manage their risks. To avoid having to resort to numbing micromanagement, regulators have increasingly insisted that banks put in place systems that allow management to have both the information and procedures to be aware of their own true risk exposures on a global basis and to be able to modify such exposures. The better these risk information and control systems, the more risk a bank can prudently assume.

In other words, if banks have better data processing systems—and guess who is the judge of that—maybe they can run their derivative bets up to $100 trillion, or maybe more!

The revolution in information and data processing technology has transformed our financial markets and the way our financial institutions conduct their operations. In most respects, these technological advances have enhanced the potential for reducing transactions costs [this does **not** mean that working people get a lower credit card interest rate or late fees or a lower home mortgage interest rate], to the benefit of consumers of financial services, and for managing risks. But in some respects they have increased the potential for more rapid and widespread disruption [such as a complete collapse of our economy].

The efficiency of global financial markets, engendered by the rapid proliferation of financial products, has the capability of transmitting mistakes [like a big losing derivative bet] at a far faster pace throughout the financial system in ways that were unknown a generation ago, and not even remotely imagined in the 19th century.[57]

As Benjamin Anderson wrote:

"Before 1913, while we were on the gold standard, none of this existed: There were no billions of dollars of 'hot money' . . . moving nervously about from one financial center to another through fear of confiscation or through fear of further currency

debasement. . . . No statesmen boasted of achievements in unbalancing the budgets or termed the deficit 'investment'. . . no country took pride in debasing its currency as a clever financial expedient."[58]

Financial crises in the early 19th century, for example, particularly those associated with the Napoleonic Wars, were often related to military and other events in faraway places. Communication was still comparatively primitive. An investor's speculative position could be wiped out by a military setback, and he might not even know about it for days or even weeks. **[But not wiped out by a "rogue" trader, such as that which occurred at Barings Brothers Bank.]**

Similarly, the collapse of Barings Brothers in 1995 showed how much more rapidly losses can be generated in the current environment relative to a century earlier when Barings Brothers confronted a similar episode.

While Mr. Nicholas Leeson, the trader who destroyed Baring's balance sheet, was winning his bets, Barings did in retrospect a poor job of supervising him. If asked, I would expect that his supervisors would have said that the bank's trading activities were "prudent" and not irresponsible. After Mr. Leeson lost, however, it turned out that his bets were "unauthorized." This is the essence of systemic risk: banks taking fantastic risks through leverage.

Current technology enables single individuals to initiate massive transactions with very rapid execution. Clearly, not only has the productivity of global finance increased markedly, but so, obviously, has the ability to generate losses at a previously inconceivable rate.

The "productivity of global finance" that Mr. Greenspan speaks of is in fact increased wealth transfer. Nothing is being produced that improves our standard of living. It is just a form of gambling by financial firms subsidized by ordinary taxpayers.

Whether we think about risk in financial markets from a national or, increasingly, international perspective, we should recognize that, if it is technology that has imparted occasional stress to markets, technology can be employed to contain it. Enhancements to financial institutions' internal risk-management systems arguably constitute one of the most effective countermeasures to the increased potential instability of the global financial system.

Question:

If the banking system has things under control, why do we need a taxpayer-funded safety net/subsidy?

The fact is that these so-called countermeasures may be totally inadequate.

Because the evolution of new technologies takes time, I suspect that we have tended to exaggerate the negative effects of information and data processing technologies on financial markets. We have focused on the ability of financial market participants to increase their leverage beyond the elusive optimum point. That is, some have voiced concern that *the subsidy embodied in the safety net has supported a greater degree of risk-taking than might be appropriate.* [Emphasis added] This is obviously a legitimate concern. [YES! YES! YES! Mr. Greenspan is telling us in very explicit terms that the safety net is a subsidy which stimulates too much risk taking!]

Nonetheless, although we may not yet fully appreciate the benefits of recent technological advances, the availability of new technology and new derivative financial instruments already has facilitated more rigorous approaches to the conceptualization, measurement, and management of risk by financial institutions. There are, of course, limitations to the statistical models used in such systems owing to the necessity of overly simplifying assumptions. [For example, using these models, both sides of a trade can show profits! Somebody has it wrong. If they get it too wrong, then ordinary working people and seniors pay the penalty.]

Question:

Are all this wealth transfer and the attendant risk along with higher interest rates fair to ordinary working people and seniors and other taxpayers?

Consequently, human judgments, based on analytically less precise but far more realistic evaluations of what the future may hold, are of critical importance in risk management. Although a sophisticated understanding of statistical modeling techniques is important to risk management, an intimate knowledge of the markets in which an institution trades, and of the customers it serves, is turning out to be far more important. [Does this mean that all of these analytics may not be that useful after all?]

The diminishing of legal, institutional, and now technological barriers to international financial activities has provided strong impetus to the process of cooperation I referred to earlier. The efforts of bank supervisors meeting at the Bank for International Settlements in Basel have been especially prominent, and deservedly so. They have set minimum standards for sound banking for the world's major banks and have sensitized all of us to the risks that banks must manage. [In other words, the BIS has set "minimum standards," we're all now "sensitized," and so everything is Ok.]

Question:

Again, why shouldn't private bankers set their own standards and make bets with their own money?

However, their work is not done. Our concepts of appropriate standards continue to evolve just as the technology of risk management evolves. In addition, supervisors from the G-10 countries must continue their efforts to bring supervisors from other countries, including the emerging and transition economies of Asia, Latin America, and Eastern Europe into the process of cooperation—both to learn from their experiences and to encourage other countries to strengthen their own supervisory systems.

Financial services

While I do not intend to say much about the provision of financial services by central banks, I might distinguish—in an oversimplified fashion—two types of functions. One includes issuing currency **[creating money out of nothing]**, acting as fiscal agent for the government **[including buying bonds issued by the government and paying for those bonds with newly-created money (monetizing debt)]**, and other functions that are reasonably straightforward and primarily, though not exclusively, domestic in character. I say straightforward, although I recognize that central bankers in Europe are devoting an extraordinary amount of effort to making sure that such functions will be performed well even as the monetary side of the European Union evolves. These are crucial functions that central banks naturally perform. Nevertheless, one should consider from time to time the extent to which the private sector could perform some of these functions more effectively. **[I suspect that he is talking about the payments clearing system, as with check clearing.]**

The other type of function relates more closely to the principal thrust of my remarks today and involves the need to ensure that the global financial system operates smoothly. What I have in mind specifically is a central bank's role in large value or interbank payment systems: on the one hand, setting standards for risk controls and monitoring the systems; on the other hand, providing certainty, or "finality," to payments made among participants in the system and, when necessary and appropriate, providing liquidity to participants [bailing banks out at taxpayer expense].

Any private bank, or for that matter any private business organization, can provide payment services with final settlement. The difficulty is that the final claim on the books of any private institution is not risk-free. Only a central bank is in a position to perform these functions under all circumstances. That, of course, is an element of the safety net [subsidy/wealth transfer], and it therefore raises the same issues of moral hazard and potential abuse of a nation's sovereign credit rating.

In fact, the amount of interbank currency transactions is on the order of $1.3 trillion per day. However, because of time zone differences, banks are never completely settled with each other every night. On weekends there are about three days' worth of unsettled transactions in the system totaling almost $4 trillion.

It is significant to understand that most of this money flow is not for goods transfer but to facilitate subsidized gambling by banks and Wall Street firms. There is no benefit to the ordinary taxpayer, and there is no reason why he should be forced by Law to subsidize it. For example, in 1997, Citibank took in more than $2 billion in revenue from "trading."[59] How did this subsidized activity help ordinary taxpayers?

The Bank for International Settlements (BIS) has stated that banks are not being mindful enough of counter-party risk, i.e., the risk that one or more banks may not be able to settle their part of a transaction (perhaps because they suffered a large loss on a derivative bet and no longer have the funds). This has the potential of cascading into a major default by other

banks in the chain of transactions. What Mr. Greenspan means is that in the event of such a failure, the Fed—read that taxpayers—would come to the rescue and supply the needed funds to those banks that cannot make good on their obligations.

To be sure, private financial institutions themselves must work to develop the infrastructure for ensuring that payments and settlements can take place with reasonable confidence and that the risks other than those absorbed by the central bank are well understood and properly managed. Those risks will not be eliminated entirely; reducing "float" in the payment system to zero, which would eliminate settlement risk, must be balanced by the capital costs of doing so.

In other words, it would cost the banks money to reduce this risk. If the Fed, along with our elected representatives with whom banks have colluded, is willing, why not pass the cost to taxpayers?

It has been just in the last year or so that the risks associated with settlement of the enormous volume of foreign exchange transactions have been fully appreciated, more than 20 years after an incident involving Bank Herstatt in Germany brought this issue to international attention. A report produced last year by a G-10 central bank committee **[This report has been kept SECRET!]** elaborated on these risks and urged the private sector to respond with appropriate institutions and risk controls.

Questions:

Why isn't there full disclosure?

Don't the people have a right to know what the risks are since they are the ones who will be called upon to absorb the losses?

I am encouraged that much progress seems to be underway in this area, as in others.

Monetary policy

This brings me, finally, to the area of monetary policy—the fundamental responsibility of a modern central bank. In this area, I am pleased to say, there have been positive developments, especially with regard to inflation. The recent record on inflation reduction in industrial countries has been impressive. Measured consumer price inflation in G-10 countries averaged only about 2-1/4 percent last year, down more than 3 percentage points from what it was in 1990. Consumer price increases on average in the G-10 have been kept under 3 percent for the past five years—the longest such period of sustained low inflation in more than three decades.

An overlooked reason that we have not been experiencing high CPI inflation, despite the fact that money creation is increasing at more than seven percent, is that many laws have been passed that persuade prudent people not to spend their money but, rather, to place it in quasi-savings plans such as IRA's, Keogh's, and 401(k)'s. By law, money placed in these quasi-savings plans must be invested in the capital markets. If the newly-created money is not spent, if it does not hit the market for final goods and services, then it does not impact the CPI. This is not something that Mr. Greenspan should be congratulating himself about.

Inflation performance in developing countries also has improved substantially. This success reflects in large part a thorough conceptual overhaul of economic thinking and policymaking. A consensus gradually emerged starting in the late 1970s that inflation destroyed jobs, or at least could not create them. This view has become particularly evident in the communiqués that have emanated from the high-level international gatherings of the past two decades.

Also, CPI inflation in the U.S. is lower than it would otherwise be as a result of foreign central bank purchases of U.S. Government securities. Since the end of 1992, they have purchased about $1 *trillion* worth. They are monetizing U.S. debt. One consequence is that instead of converting dollars accumulating from the U.S. trade deficit, now on the order of $400 billion per year and increasing, into their own currencies, they are maintaining a stronger dollar than it would otherwise be. This has the effect of keeping their currencies relatively weaker. It has enabled foreigners to export more to the U.S. At the same time, this facilitates job transfer from the U.S. to other countries.

On information and belief, about 28% of U.S. consumer purchases are from imports. Because of foreign central bank dollar intervention, imports are less expensive than they would otherwise be. Not only does this cause our CPI to be lower, it prevents U.S. manufacturers of competitive goods from raising prices, thereby denying them pricing power. This, in turn, causes the CPI to be even lower still.

Further, because the CPI is perceived as low and trending lower, interest rates, which include a CPI inflation premium, are also lower than they would otherwise be. In turn, lower interest rates enable the banking system to increase leverage further by lending to more marginal (less credit-worthy) borrowers. A side effect is that the earnings of publicly-traded companies are capitalized at a higher value. This induces people to bid up stock prices. The increase in equity valuations facilitates even more lending.

Foreign central banks have accumulated more than $1 trillion of U.S. Treasuries. There is no precedent when poorer foreign governments have funded a richer government in this way. Historically, the only way a government could get money from foreign governments was to conquer them and then collect money as tribute.

Another way of looking at this is that foreigners are now supplying U.S. citizens with about $400 billion per year in goods and services in return for irredeemable-paper-ticket or electronic-checkbook fiat money (dollars). Since it costs almost nothing to produce fiat money, as a society, we have been getting those goods and services virtually for free.

No wonder the CPI inflation index has stayed low. No wonder so many jobs have migrated to foreign shores. If the shoe were on the other foot, i.e., if a Japanese person spent yen in America, then as fast as an eyeblink those yen would be converted to dollars.

Also, it is significant that foreigners with their own money are not making the ongoing purchases of U.S. Treasuries. Foreign governmental agencies are doing the purchasing with someone else's money, and for political purposes.

We should take care, however, that our recent success not make us complacent. It is becoming increasingly evident that a key ingredient in achieving the highest possible levels of productivity, real incomes, and living standards over the long run is maintenance of price stability.

The notion that price stability is desirable will not stand careful scrutiny. As mentioned earlier, as people acquire new and better skills, as manufacturing processes improve, as capital is invested in plant and equipment, quality improves and prices *decline*. This is the history of the world. There is virtually nothing that doesn't get better and cheaper over time. That is what an increasing standard of living means: more goods for more people at cheaper prices. To create just enough new money so that prices stay stable is to deny ordinary working people and seniors an increase in their living standard.

But to sustain good inflation performance, we need to understand the other factors that lie behind our recent success, in addition to the policy consensus of governments, which must not be allowed to ebb as memories of the stagflation in the 1970s fade. Internally, various steps are being implemented that free up markets and intensify competition, not just in product markets, but in labor markets and financial sectors as well. On the external side, emerging nations, especially in Asia and Latin America, have become increasingly important as production sites and markets and thus as competitors. Faced with this broadened foreign competition, firms in many countries now find it less easy than in the past to raise prices during periods of rising demand at home.

The process of adjustment has not been entirely painless. Industrial economies in particular are going through an extended period of economic and financial restructuring that has hit some sectors, firms, and groups of workers particularly hard. The fact that in the past these groups may have felt insulated from such forces probably heightened the consequent stress, and may have contributed to some general uncertainty and insecurity. As a result, workers at present, to a greater extent than usual, trade aspirations for higher levels of earnings for job security.

67

The effect of foreigners accepting fiat money in exchange for their goods and services undercuts ordinary working people in our home market. If we had honest money, such as gold, this would not be possible.

Clearly it takes some time for an economy to realize the full benefits of transition from a high—or even moderate-inflation environment—with associated uncertainties about future inflation—to one where inflation is low and under control. Inflation expectations throughout the economy must fall, and financial-market premia related to inflation uncertainty have to dissipate.

I doubt the tasks of central bankers will become any easier as we move into the 21st century. Clearly price stability should and will remain the central goal of our activities.

But, creating just enough money to ensure price stability deprives ordinary working people and seniors of the benefits they would get if prices decreased. Again, the purchasing power of savings should increase.

But we are having increasing difficulty in pinning down the notion of what constitutes a stable price level. When industrial product was the centerpiece of the advanced economies during the first two-thirds of this century, our overall price indexes served us well. Pricing a pound of electrolytic copper presented few definitional problems. The price of a ton of cold rolled steel sheet, or a linear yard of cotton broad woven fabric, could be reasonably compared over a period of years.

Mr. Greenspan may be making a conceptual error here. The CPI inflation index is supposed to measure price changes in *final* goods sold to consumers. Electrolytic copper, cold rolled steel and yards of cotton broad woven fabric are *intermediate* goods which are not measured by the CPI. It is significant to note that the

prices of these kinds of industrial products have decreased and their quality has improved. One would expect, then, that prices of products made with these goods also to decrease in price and improve in quality.

But as the century draws to a close, the simple notion of price has turned decidedly ambiguous. What is the price of a unit of software or a legal opinion? How does one evaluate the change in the price of a cataract operation over a ten-year period when the nature of the procedure and its impact on the patient has changed so radically? Indeed, how will we measure inflation, and the associated financial and real implications, in the 21st century when our data—using current techniques—could become increasingly less adequate to trace price trends over time?

In other words, the CPI is not meaningful. To paraphrase, over time almost all products change and the original products disappear from the market. So measuring the prices of a fixed basket of goods, much of which has been replaced by newer and better product and is therefore obsolete, has no information value. Further, creating money has implications other than CPI inflation: it affects the equity markets, interest rates, the investment-time-horizon, real estate prices and many other factors.

So long as individuals make contractual arrangements for future payments valued in dollars, or marks, or francs, there must be a presumption on the part of those involved in the transaction about the future purchasing power of money. [YES!] No matter how complex individual products become, there will always be some general sense of the purchasing power of money both across time and across goods and services.

Hence, we must assume that embodied in all products is some unit of output and hence of price that is recognizable to producers and consumers and upon which they will base their decisions. Doubtless, we will develop new techniques of price measurement to unearth them as the years go on. It is crucial that we do, for inflation can destabilize an economy even if faulty price indexes fail to reveal it. **[In other words, we can have very serious problems even if the CPI stays quiescent.]**

However such conceptual and technical issues are resolved, central bankers need to err on the side of caution. Working in the context of our individual political environments, we are the ultimate protectors and preservers of the value of our currencies.

Here, Mr. Greenspan is saying that the Federal Reserve is not "independent" at all, but must work within the context, i.e., constraints, of its "political environment." When I had my first brief conversation with him in 1993, during which time he told me that he "absolutely" agreed with the reasoning and conclusions in his "Gold and Economic Freedom" article, I asked him why he didn't speak out.

He said at the time: "Because my colleagues at the institution I represent disagree with me." So, I conclude that "working in the context of . . . political environments" appears to mean to him that he must keep truth to himself. Nevertheless, he is clearly saying things that emphasize the unfairness and perils of our current fiat money system and the merits of resuming gold-as-money.

A central banker cannot be exempted from one very basic fact: In the long run inflation is essentially a monetary phenomenon. **[YES! Inflation results from creating money, plain and simple.]** Accordingly, the best approach is to maintain a steady course with an appropriate level of restraint.

NO! The best approach is to: (1) stop transferring wealth from seniors and workers to banks and to Wall Street firms; (2) ensure a monetary system with the lowest possible interest rate and the highest number of jobs; (3) remove uncertainty as to the efficacy of money for long-term investments and savings; (4) insulate the country from the possibility of a catastrophic currency meltdown; (5) reign in runaway spending by the Congress; and, (6) stabilize currency transactions between nations. All of this may be accomplished by resuming gold-as-money, the historic and clear choice of the people. Of course, under these circumstances there would be much less of a need for central banks, and banks and Wall Street firms would play a much-abbreviated role in our society.

Countries whose currencies are widely used internationally, like the United States, have a special responsibility to provide an anchor of stability for themselves and the world at large.

Conclusion

In conclusion, let me bring together three aspects of central bank responsibilities. Monetary policy must aim to provide a stable macroeconomic environment, to promote sustainable long-term economic growth without inflation and to allow financial markets to operate without excessive uncertainty. Central banks provide direct support to financial markets through their role in the safety net, that is, the extension to the financial system, under certain circumstances, of the nation's sovereign credit rating. This element of subsidy requires a degree of supervision and regulation to ensure that the safety net is not abused. The payment system, and the central banks' involvement in it, is a key element of the safety net and is, as well, at the core of the financial system through which monetary policy is implemented.

Central banks, like everyone else, operate in a global financial market. I can say with some confidence that everywhere, not just in Europe, the concept of a domestic market will have even less meaning in a decade than it does today. It is much more difficult to predict what the world will look like in all its dimensions, but my hope and expectation is that central banks will play a positive part. As all industrial countries are likely to experience similar forces, cooperation is key to our continued success.

End Notes

[1]The phrase "lender of last resort" is double speak. The concept of "lending" implies that money lent is expected to be paid back in money that has the same purchasing power as the money "lent." This is not the case. The essence of the arrangement is that ordinary taxpayers replenish banks' balance sheets. It is wealth transfer, plain and simple.

[2] See: Parks, Lawrence M.; "Currency Debasement: Its Effect on the World Economy;" Monograph # 52; Committee for Monetary Research and Education, Inc., Charlotte, North Carolina, June 1996.

[3] People generally do not understand that banks become debtors (borrowers) when they accept deposits. Deposits made by the public go on banks' balance sheets as liabilities, that is, something they owe. Mr. Greenspan is explaining that the government "stands ready to guarantee" those obligations. Also, when banks extend credit, they *create* a deposit, which is the same as creating money. Banking jargon for creating deposits is called "fractional reserve lending."

[4] Throughout this speech, Mr. Greenspan makes references to banks and other financial institutions. Keep in mind that he is speaking mostly about large money center banks. Smaller banks do not enjoy the same special treatment that their larger competitors receive.

[5] These days, U.S. banks seek to avoid having to sell to the Federal Reserve bad foreign loans and other non-performing "assets," e.g., money that the Bank of Korea owes JP Morgan for having lost a derivative bet. Instead, they seek to have the International Monetary Fund (IMF), another taxpayer-funded entity, advance money to foreign debtors who then transmit that money (as repayment) to U.S. banks. This works out better for U.S. banks since all of the agreements that the IMF has consummated with foreign debtors are kept secret. There is no disclosure even though U.S. taxpayers are advancing billions. In 1997, for example, U.S. and foreign workers transferred more than $100 billion to foreign banks through the IMF.

[6] Vieira, Edwin Jr., "The Federal Reserve System: A Fatal Parasite on the American Body Politic"; National Alliance for Constitutional Money, Manassas, Virginia; Monograph #4. Full text is available on FAME's Internet website: www.fame.org.

[7] Pringle, Robert; and Deane, Marjorie: *The Central Banks*; Viking, 1994, page viii.

[8] Smithers, Andrew; "Halt subsidized debt to damp down the flames of Asian contagion," *Business Day*, March 30, 1998.

[9] Greenspan, Alan; "Gold and Economic Freedom", Rand, Ayn; *Capitalism: the Unknown Ideal*; Signet Books, 1967; pp96-101.

[10] Federal Reserve Bank of Richmond 1996 Annual Report; page 5.

[11] Perhaps Mr. Greenspan's reference to creating "claims" is his way of letting us know that money created by the banking system is not wealth. Wealth cannot be created without work. It is that which remains after one consumes what one produces. How much more work is required to create a $100 bill as opposed to a $1 bill? The money being created by the banking system may possibly be exchanged for wealth at a future time, provided that people continue to assign value to it, and in that sense one might think of money as a potential "claim."

[12] Citizens for Budget Reform has developed a balance sheet for the U.S. Government showing the present value of all contingent liabilities. According to them, those liabilities approach $50 trillion! See their website http://www.budget.org/USABIS for more information.

[13] With our system, the government itself does not create money. Fiat money creation, which is not a power granted to the Congress under the *Constitution*, has been somehow delegated to the banking system. Mindful of how diligent the defenders of the Rule of Law are when it comes to condemning unconstitutional legislation that favors ordinary working people, why are they not loudly objecting when ordinary working people are being ripped off?

[14] Greenspan, Alan: "Gold and Economic Freedom;" in Rand, Ayn; *Capitalism: the Unknown Ideal*; Signet Books, 1967; pp96-101.

[15] Fisher, Kenneth L.; *The Wall Street Waltz: 90 Visual Perspectives*; Contemporary Books, Inc.; Chicago; 1987, page 111.

[16] The "crowding out" hypothesis has come under attack by those who point to the fact that interest rates dropped during the Reagan years while government borrowing increased markedly. Thus, critics say, there is no "crowding out" effect. The response is that, with a fiat money system, provided that newly-created money does not hit the goods and services market where it would affect the CPI, interest rates tend to fall. Once the CPI is impacted, however, interest rates rise with a vengeance, and commercial arrangements that were predicated on lower interest rates collapse.

[17] Burstein, Melvin; Executive Vice President and General Counsel, Federal Reserve Bank of Minneapolis, Vol 7, "Is deposit insurance the banker's Faustian bargain?" *Fedgazette* 1/1/95 page 14.

[18] In the last few years, a high percentage of money created by banks has gone for merger & acquisition activities. Since most of that money ends up in the hands of very few people, very little of it gets spent into the consumer goods market, thereby leaving the CPI quiescent. Most of the newly-created money gets funneled into the capital markets which increase the stock market bubble.

[19] With a fiat monetary system, ordinary working people lose no matter what. If interest rates are *not* "allowed to rise," then inflation increases, workers' pensions and savings lose purchasing power, and workers are exposed to systemic risk—the risk that the entire monetary edifice will crash. Alternatively, if interest rates *are* "allowed to rise," then jobs get snuffed out.

[20] Brauer, David A.; "Do Rising Labor Costs Trigger Higher Inflation?" - *Current Issues in Economics and Finance*, Vol 3 Number 11, September 1997, Federal Reserve Bank of New York.

[21] Perhaps the wages in the service sector are going up faster than those in the manufacturing sector because manufacturing is vulnerable to competition from overseas while services generally are not.

[22] Source: Federal Reserve Flow of Funds Reports, Federal Reserve Statistical Release Z.1, June 8, 2001, series L.109 Commercial Banking, page 69.

[23] If the banks did not have a monopoly on the creation of fiat money, if the government itself created money, which is not something this author favors, then at least taxpayers would not have to pay "interest" to banks for money banks create on behalf of the government.

[24] This is a complete misstatement. The principal form of leverage in which banks engage is not "taking deposits," as Mr. Greenspan suggests. It is in creating deposits, a process called "fractional reserve lending."

[25] Skousen, Mark; *Economics of a Pure Gold Standard*; The Foundation for Economic Education, Irvington-on-Hudson, New York, 1996, 3rd Edition, page 23.

[26] This concept appears confusing mostly because it is blatantly outrageous. Banks have been empowered to perform an act, which if performed by an ordinary person, would be considered fraud!

[27] Federal Reserve publications (e.g., "The Story of Money," Federal Reserve Bank of New York, 1997, page 23) explain the process in a very confusing way. However, they do say: ". . . the banking system actually creates money." They go on to say that this is "complicated" and that Congress has delegated regulation of this function to the Federal Reserve.

[28] Citibank recently sent out notices to its depositors to the effect that they may not receive their money on demand but may have to wait a week if Citibank needs extra time to make good. Source: Citibank notice "Information about Business Checking Accounts" Effective March 16, 1998.

[29] As of 8/31/93, on transaction deposits less than $43.3 million, the reserve requirement was 3 percent; on transaction deposits more than $43.3 million, the reserve requirement was 10 percent; and on savings and time deposits, there has been no reserve requirement since 1991.

Mr. Franklin Sanders, editor of *The Moneychanger*, reports a conversation on 8/31/93 with Alton Gilbert of the Federal Reserve Bank of St. Louis confirming the following as of May, 1993: (all amounts in billions)

Total Required Reserves:	$55.1
M3 (M2 + large denomination time deposits)	4,171.0
Less: M2 money market funds	-336.5
M3 money market funds	-202.8
M2 currency	-304.0
Total bank and S&L deposits	3,327.7

$$\frac{\text{Reserve}}{\text{Requirement}} = \frac{\text{Total Required Reserve (55.1)}}{\text{Total Deposits (3,327.7)}} = 1.66\%$$

Therefore, for every $1 that the Federal Reserve creates out of nothing, the banking system can create an additional $60.

[30] Rothbard, Murray N.; *The Case Against The Fed*; The Ludwig von Mises Institute; Auburn, Alabama, 1994, pp33ff.

[31] Vieira, Edwin Jr., "The Federal Reserve System: A Fatal Parasite on the American Body Politic"; National Alliance for Constitutional Money, Manassas, Virginia; Monograph #4. Full text is available on FAME's Internet website: www.fame.org.

[32] Skousen, Mark; *Economics of a Pure Gold Standard*; The Foundation for Economic Education, Irvington-on-Hudson, New York, 1996, 3rd Edition, page 22ff.

[33] Skousen, Mark; *Economics of a Pure Gold Standard*; The Foundation for Economic Education, Irvington-on-Hudson, New York, 1996, 3rd Edition, page 23.

[34] Because the bad loans could not be repaid or sold, it was mostly the good loans that were called. Thus, good businesses were deprived of credit, and many of them failed as a result.

[35] Radio Address of the President, May 7, 1933; Outlining the New Deal Program - Fireside Chat #2.

[36] March 12, 1933. Address of President Roosevelt by radio, delivered from the President's Study in the White House at 10 P.M.

[37] For an explanation of Mr. Greenspan's analysis of the cause of the Great Depression, see: Greenspan, Alan; "Gold and Economic Freedom" in Rand, Ayn; *Capitalism the Unknown Ideal*; Signet Books, 1967, pp96-101.

[38] When the Federal Reserve and the Treasury used the "Exchange Stabilization Fund" to bail out Mexico in 1995, the money supplied to Mexico was quickly transferred to the Wall Street firms and banks that had purchased Mexican securities. What happened was that U.S. financial institutions, ignoring the fact that every so often the Mexican peso melts, in an effort to garner extra yield, bought Mexican securities. When it appeared certain that Mexican debt would default, rather than allow these financial institutions to book a loss, our government—read that ordinary taxpayers—lent money to Mexico so that it could repay U.S. banks and Wall Street firms. Another version of this story is being played out by the International

Monetary Fund, in part financed by U.S. taxpayers, to bail out banks in South Korea, Indonesia, Malaysia, the Philippines, and elsewhere.

[39] See Greenspan, Alan; "Gold and Economic Freedom;" in Rand, Ayn; *Capitalism the Unknown Ideal*; Signet Books, 1967, pp96-101.

[40] Defenders of the Rule of Law properly condemn much of the New Deal Legislation that the representatives of ordinary working people perceive as beneficial. How come they aren't equally energized when ordinary working people are being victimized?

[41] Vieira, Edwin Jr.; *The Texas Review of Law & Politics*; Vol. 2, No. 1, Fall 1997; "The Forgotten Role of The Constitution in Monetary Law." Full text is available on FAME's Internet website: www.fame.org.

[42] Rothbard, Murray N.; *Making Economic Sense*; Ludwig von Mises Institute, 1995, pp284.

[43] *Grant's Interest Rate Observer*, March 28, 1997, page 7 reported that the notional value of derivatives as $21 trillion. Grant's source was the International Swaps and Derivatives Association. However, according the *Economist Newspaper*, in an article entitled "System Failure" by Martin Giles, Vol. 339, 4/27/96 page 5, "Commercial banks are also heavily engaged in over-the-counter (OTC) derivatives (i.e., those that are not traded on a recognized exchange). A survey of the market published under the auspices of the Bank for International Settlements showed that, at the end of March 1995, the total amount of outstanding OTC contracts had reached an eye-popping $41 trillion." A recent article in *Forbes*, "Who needs derivatives?" by Carolyn T. Geer, April 21, 1997, page 52, put the derivatives market at more than $60 trillion in notional principal.

[44] See: Dowd, Kevin; *Laissez-faire Banking*; Routledge Publishing, New York, 1993, pp297.

[45] Buffett, Howard: "Human Freedom Rests on Gold Redeemable Money"; 1948; From *The Commercial and Financial Chronicle*, 5/6/48; (FAME is indebted to the Committee for Monetary Research

and Education for bringing Mr. Buffett's speech to our attention.) Complete text is available on FAME's Internet website: www.FAME.org in the Publications section.

[46] Greider, William, *Secrets of the Temple*, Simon & Schuster 1987, pp89.

[47] Federal Reserve Board of Governor Lawrence Lindsey, Federal Open Market Operations Meeting, June 30, 1992 as quoted by *FOMC Alert*, March 31, 1998 - Financial Markets Center, Philomont, Virginia 20131.

[48] Schroeder, Michael, "Law That Separates Banks, Brokers Always Seems to Find Patron in Time," *The Wall Street Journal*, April 10, 1998.

[49] Davies, Stephen A.; "Some Lawmakers Claim Federal Reserve Keeps Critics at Bay With Jobs", *The American Banker*Bond Buyer*, December 2, 1994 page 3.

[50] Rothbard, Murray N.; *The Case Against the Fed*; Ludwig Von Mises Institute, 1994, pp97ff.

[51] For a compelling analysis of why people choose gold as money see: Fekete, Antal E.; "Whither Gold"; available on FAME's Internet Website http://www.fame.org. "Whither Gold" was the winner of the International Currency Prize in 1996, sponsored by Bank Lips Ltd., Zurich, Switzerland.

[52] The "money issue" dominated 19th Century politics in the U.S. It was continually discussed in newspapers and elsewhere. Major political battles were fought over it from the time of the Revolution until World War I.

[53] For an exhaustive review of the constitutional issues relating to gold see: Vieira, Edwin Jr.: *Pieces of Eight: The Monetary Powers And Disabilities Of The U.S. Constitution*; Sound Dollar Committee - 1983 and also "The Forgotten Role of the Constitution in Monetary Law" - *The Texas Review of Law & Politics*, Vol. 2, No.1, Fall 1997 pp77-128.

[54] See: Unger, Irwin; *The Greenback Era*, Princeton University Press, 1961.

[55] March 12, 1933. Address of President Roosevelt by radio, delivered from the President's Study in the White House at 10 P.M.

[56] Pringle, Robert; and Deane, Marjorie; *The Central Banks* - Viking, 1994, Page vii.

[57] The "proliferation of financial products" is another symptom of our fiat money system. It used to be that product innovation meant improvements in the stuff that we use in our daily lives that raised our standard of living.

[58] Anderson, Benjamin M.; *Economics and the Public Welfare*, D. Van Nostrand, 1949, as quoted by the Committee for Monetary Research and Education.

[59] See: Citicorp Annual Report 1997, page 50.

Epilogue

My face-to-face (brief) conversations with Mr. Greenspan

On two occasions, I have met face-to-face with Mr. Greenspan. Each encounter lasted just a few minutes, and they were both after he had addressed the Economic Club of New York, of which I am a member. Consisting mostly of financial sector participants, which is to be expected in New York City, Economic Club meetings where Mr. Greenspan has spoken generally draw upwards of 2,000 people. The meetings, which are gala dinner or luncheon affairs at the New York Hilton, also serve as networking opportunities. Mr. Greenspan has addressed this group an unprecedented six times.

When he comes to these events, Mr. Greenspan travels without an entourage, and he carries his own briefcase. He is approachable and friendly, although at the last event he literally bolted at the conclusion, quickly alighting the stairs at the back of the Hilton's main ballroom, where he got into an elevator and withdrew to his suite.

On April 19, 1993, which was prior to my forming FAME, I approached Mr. Greenspan as he came off the dais, and complemented him profusely on an article he wrote in 1966 titled "Gold and Economic Freedom." The article can be found in a book called *Capitalism the Unknown Ideal*, which is an anthology of essays, mostly by Ayn Rand. I inquired whether I could ask him some questions about the article. Digressing for a moment, in this article, Mr. Greenspan took the position that gold-as-money is a precondition for a free society, something we all presumably are in favor of. When I mentioned the article, he told me that coincidentally he had recently reread it.

During the small talk portion of our conversation, five times he asked me if I was with the press, and each time I said "no." Finally he said, "So what is your question?" I said, "Do you still agree with the reasoning and the conclusions in this article?" His response was an emphatic "Absolutely!" Then, I asked, "So why don't you speak out?" Mr. Greenspan said: "Because my colleagues at the institution I represent disagree with me." [Note the absence of proper nouns.] And I responded, "But you know where all of this is leading to [a complete collapse]." He then gave me a very pained look, like I had punched him in the stomach, and walked on.

The second time I approached him, which was on January 13, 2000, I was waiting for him as he alighted the stairs to leave the Hilton's main ballroom. Again, we had some pleasantries, and I asked him what the moral justification was for legal tender laws. He gave me a very convoluted nonsensical (to me) answer that I believe he knew made no sense. We spoke briefly about the merits of gold-as-money, with which he concurred, and then I asked him why, if he understands what is happening and what the implications are, he doesn't speak out more. His answer had a ring of truth and, also, a tinge of desperation. He said: "Nobody wants to hear it." By then, we had reached the elevators on the floor above the main ballroom, and he got in with his wife, Andrea Mitchell, who was most charming.

As one might imagine, I continue to have mixed feelings about Mr. Greenspan's role in the monetary system. On one hand, he heads a *prima facie* evil institution that I believe he must understand is evil. On the other hand, in contrast to all of his predecessors, he has been fairly open—but not completely open—about the flaws in our monetary system. Could he do more to set things right? The answer, at least to me, is an unequivocal "Yes."

Attempting to look at the situation from his point of view, one should note that he is 75 years old and has no children. For him, as he states in the beginning of the Leuven speech, the long term is two years. One is reminded of comments attributed to George Washington, who, after sitting through the Constitutional Convention, and knowing full well the flaws in the *Constitution*, especially chattel slavery, is reported to have said something to the effect that this was the best that could be done under the circumstances—Washington was concerned that if the Colonies did not unite that they would be vulnerable to attack from France and/or Britain—and that future generations would have to work things out. In a similar way, Mr. Greenspan may feel that he has done all he can. To his credit, Mr. Greenspan has shown us some of the markers. It is up to us to follow his lead.

Anecdotal evidence of impending collapse

All around the world, fiat money monetary systems are collapsing or have collapsed: Russia, Peru, the Philippines, Malaysia, Indonesia, Brazil, South Korea, Turkey, Mexico, and elsewhere. If one thinks of America as the center of empire, then the empire is collapsing around the periphery, and the periphery is getting closer. Those who are in control—"control" may not be the right word, because, at the end of the day they will be shown to be impotent—of our monetary system understand about the risks of systemic collapse, although they have shielded their eyes from the most important evidence. When they attend industry conferences, they talk about it all the time. In this respect, Mr. Greenspan is not alone.

It has gotten to the point where the "authorities" are attempting to shore up international institutions in order to deal with the cataclysm that they all know is coming. Recall then Secretary of the Treasury Larry Summers frantically importuning the bolstering of the balance sheet of the International Monetary Fund (the "IMF"). In effect, the IMF plays the role of "lender of last resort" to the international community, transferring the wealth of ordinary people to banks in other countries so they may make good to (mostly) U.S. banks.

More to the point, the Bank for International Settlements (the "BIS") has recently formed the Financial Stability Institute and the Financial Stability Forum. The BIS did not form these entities because everything is fine. They know they have a problem. Similarly, the Council on Foreign Relations (the "CFR") has recently hosted simulation games on financial collapse. Again, the top people understand there is a problem, otherwise, why bother?

About three years ago, a hedge fund called Long Term Capital Management ("LTCM"), which was capitalized with a mere $3 billion, put, we were told by then Secretary of Treasury Robert Rubin, then President Clinton, et. al., the world's entire financial structure at risk! How could that be? It turned out that LTCM had leveraged its balance sheet more than a hundred times and that its counterparties, which in some cases included *central banks*—in effect those central banks were gambling with the patrimony of their citizens—as well as banks, could have been destroyed had LTCM gone bust. That the Congress and the Establishment press did not make more of this is a scandal, in my view.

Consider, suppose you were traveling cross-country on a Boeing 767 and, somehow, conversations in the cockpit got piped into the main cabin and you heard the pilots talking about the possibility of crashing. I would be very distressed, and I expect that everyone on the plane would feel similarly. So, how come, when supposedly faced with a complete collapse of the world's financial structure people were so sanguine? Could it be that they have been so dumbed down by what they learn in government schools that they have no idea of the issues? As Martin Mayer, the brilliant Resident Scholar at the Brookings Institute points out in his new book, *The FED*, "For newspaper editors, a story about bids drying up in the bond market is what William Safire was the first to call MEGO (for My Eyes Glaze Over); for television producers, there is absolutely no redeeming social value in trying to tell about a financial crisis that has not yet punished telegenic people."[1]

The loss of knowledge is palpable. For example, on June 3, 1998, I attended an event hosted by the Economic Club of New York where one of the presenters was Mr. Alex Trottman, then Chairman and Chief Executive Officer of the Ford Motor Company. During the meet-and-greet session, I gave him my elevator speech about FAME. When I finished, he said to me: "What's fiat money?" I was flabbergasted! It is symptomatic that one of the most powerful businessmen in the world did not even know basic monetary terminology. It was not always thus.

In 1933, when President Roosevelt seized the gold belonging to citizens—an act that the late Philip Carret, then a FAME Trustee, called the "True Day of Infamy"—Roosevelt explained his actions to the general public in his first Fireside Chat. Roosevelt was a superb wordsmith; he did not use jargon. He spoke to the people using terminology and metaphors that everyone understood. He said: "This currency [after there was no longer any redeemability into gold] will not be fiat." So, at least then, everyone must have known the term. How is it today that there is such widespread ignorance about monetary terminology?

The financial sector is consuming your savings and your pension

One of the sub-headings on the FAME website (www.FAME.org) in the What's New section, deals with what I call misinformation and disinformation. The most significant misinformation promulgated by Wall Street firms—are they liable for this under our nation's securities laws? —and the Establishment press is what constitutes "wealth." Wealth is what is left over after one consumes what one produces. It is a balance sheet item, and it takes work to produce it.

Fiat money, e.g., "dollars," or securities denominated in "dollars," because there is no work involved in producing it, do not constitute wealth. After all, how much more work is required to produce a $100 bill as compared to a $1 bill? If it did not take work to produce wealth, then it would be possible to alleviate poverty worldwide overnight.

The best that can be said about fiat money or securities (think of your IRA, your Keogh, the assets in your pension plan, etc.) denominated in fiat "dollars" is that they are a *potential* claim on wealth. That is not the same thing as wealth. Again, I am indebted to Mr. Greenspan for his use of the term "creation of claims" throughout his Leuven speech. All over the world, ordinary people receive fiat money—designated "legal tender"—for their labors.

They have a problem, which is part of the human condition: how to provide for themselves in old age. As the classic labor song relates: "Too old to work, too young to die, how am I going to get by?" The answer is that one saves, and, then, when one gets old and can no longer work, one draws on one's savings. There is a presumption that one's savings consist of wealth.

In the case of the fiat money, banks, which create the fiat money when they extend credit, and Wall Street firms, which get transaction fees for moving it around, spend/convert their fees into real wealth *now*! Their principals are the ones who are buying 300-foot boats, 30,000-foot houses, $30,000 dresses (no typo) at Bergdorf's Plaza Boutique, and multimillion-dollar apartments in Donald Trump's World Tower. In effect, they are *consuming* other people's life savings! Meanwhile, ordinary people are saving fiat money and securities denominated in the fiat money for *later*, when they retire.

As we are witnessing all over the world, when later comes, it turns out that the potential claims have lost their purchasing power. In other words, the scam works because of a timing difference. It is helped along by laws (who do you suppose lobbies for these laws with "campaign contributions?") that persuade otherwise prudent people to save, e.g., IRA, Keogh (and perhaps soon the so-called "privatization" of Social Security), fiat dollars. By law, people's savings must be "invested" in the capital markets. When the time comes to draw down on their supposed "wealth," it turns out that they are left holding an empty bag.

What happens? If you are a senior, and your savings and your pension become worthless, how do you live? The answer is: you don't. You die. Recently, I hosted a talk by Dr. Paul Klebnikov, a senior editor at *Forbes*, and the author of *Godfather of the Kremlin: Boris Berezovsky and the Looting of Russia*. During his presentation, he noted that longevity in Russia has decreased five years for men and four years for women. Is there a connection between this loss of life and the loss of value of the savings and pensions of Russian workers? What is their recourse? Have you seen anything in the Establishment press or on television dealing with this issue?

Need for stability, financial sector conflict of interest

All over the world, ordinary people, small countries, and companies engaged in international trade want monetary stability. A world monetary structure where there is volatility in the major currencies, e.g., the dollar vs. the yen, the dollar vs. the euro, the yen vs. the euro, on the order of 30% to 50% over a year or two is simply unacceptable. The reason it is unacceptable is that profit margins are not great enough to absorb currency volatility of this magnitude. The financial sector, because it makes so much money on "trading," wants volatility (within limits), not stability. Thus, the financial sector has a *conflict of interest* with all of the other parties. Unfortunately, for almost all of the twentieth century, the financial sector has been *de facto* in charge of the monetary structure. In effect, they have rigged the structure for their own benefit to the detriment of everyone else.

As former Federal Reserve Chairman Paul Volcker has said, a world economy requires a world currency. What is that currency going to be? Shall it be a paper-ticket-electronic fiat currency created out of nothing by a specially privileged elite who force it on the world through a combination of legal tender laws, misrepresentations and nondisclosure? Or, shall it be the choice of free men operating in free markets with full disclosure, no misrepresentations, and no legal tender, a.k.a. "forced tender" laws?

Our hero in the Congress

While almost all of the Congress is not mindful of fiat money or have any understanding of the implications, there is one member who does understand and who has been steadfast in attempting to promote an honest monetary system. That man is Representative Ron Paul of Texas. Dr. Paul is qualitatively different from most of the other members of Congress in that he has a real profession other than politics: he is a gynecologist/obstetrician, and he has delivered 4,000 babies. Perhaps because he has a real profession and is not totally dependent upon being elected, he speaks his mind. As one might expect, he receives not a penny in contributions from the banks even though he serves on the House Banking Committee.

Message for politicians

While some politicians may benefit in the short run from "campaign contributions" denominated in fiat money, when that fiat money finally collapses, they, along with the government, will be discredited. In almost 100% of the cases, when fiat money fails, there is a regime change. People associated with the old government lose the respect of the people and that they are supposed to govern, and they are turned out.

In the 19th century, those politicians associated with sound money were triumphant. Even President Roosevelt, prior to seizing the nation's gold, made campaign speeches affirming his desire for a sound currency. Without those assurances, it is doubtful that he would have been elected.

In recent times, as reported by the *New York Times* in Turkey after the Turkish lira began its swan dive, for example, "Distrust of the government is high. If elections were held today, no established party, including the three that make up the current government, would get enough votes to sit in Parliament, according to a recent nationwide poll."[2]

The solution

The problem of fiat money is one that has confronted society time and again for the last three hundred years. In every case, one of the most spectacular being the collapse of France during John Law's tenure, the purchasing power of fiat money has approached its cost of production, which, for paper money, is near zero, and, for bank deposits, which are created when banks extend credit, is zero. How do the purveyors of fiat money get away with this, and what is to be done?

In the coming months, FAME will launch the Global Currency Initiative™, which is a study group for some of the largest industrial companies in the world. These firms, like almost everyone else on the planet, seek monetary stability for cross border transactions. They want to minimize the costs associated with myriad currencies. However, the costs that they seek to minimize are revenues to the financial sector.

Thus, the financial sector, which, to repeat, has been in *de facto* charge of the monetary structure for virtually the entire 20th century, has a *conflict of interests* with virtually everyone else: ordinary people; small countries; and, industrial firms. For this reason financial sector firms will not be participating in the Global Currency Initiative™.

What you can do to help

To change the system, there will need to be legislation. But before that happens, there needs to be more disclosure, more understanding, especially among ordinary people. You can help by sending a copy of this book to your friends, colleagues and relatives, and, at every opportunity, by asking your elected representatives:

> *"If our money is good money and would be preferred by the people, then why do we need legal tender laws? And, if our money is not good, why in a democracy should we be forced to use it?"*

---

[1] Mayer, Martin; *The Fed*, The Free Press, New York 2001, Page 14.
[2] Frantz, Douglas, "Great Divide Widens as Economy Worsens," *The New York Times*, 7/21/01 page A4.

Glossary

Term	Meaning
Bailment	Transferring property to another without transferring ownership. The bailee, the one who accepts the transfer, becomes a trustee, i.e., a custodian or a fiduciary, for the property.
Bailout	Wealth transfer, generally from ordinary people to richer people. Most bailouts occur in the financial sector for the benefit of people engaged mostly in banking.
Barter	A system of trading particular goods for other particular goods.
Call Loan	Call loans allow bankers to demand repayment "on demand." These are made mainly to brokers and security dealers.
"Cleaning Up The Mess"	A euphemism for bailing out a business (almost always a bank). The bailout is the equivalent of wealth transfer, almost always from poorer people to richer people.
Closing the 'Gold Window'	Default by the U.S. on August 15, 1971 on its sovereign promise to redeem "dollars" at the rate of one ounce of gold for 35 "dollars."

Term	Meaning
Commercial Paper	A type of loan that is generally short-term, e.g. 90 days.
Credit Reserve Standard	The dollar as the reserve currency.
Debasement	Mixing gold to be used in gold coins with a base metal, such as lead or copper, and then passing the coins as if the purity of gold was higher. Debasement is a form of devaluation and is *prima facie* fraudulent.
Deposit (as in a "bank deposit")	An unsecured loan to a bank. Sometimes the bank itself *creates* the deposit by extending credit. By law, only banks are allowed to create deposits, a special privilege that only banks (and the Federal Reserve) have.
Devaluation	Reducing the promised exchange ratio of a currency for a given commodity or other currency.
Eurodollars	Deposits of U.S. dollars in foreign banks or in overseas branches of U.S. banks.
Federal Funds Rate	The federal funds rate is the interest rate at which depository institutions (banks) lend balances at the Federal Reserve to other depository institutions (banks) overnight.

Term	Meaning
Federal Open Market Operations	The purchase or sale of an asset, which is usually a U.S. Government Security, by the Federal Reserve. When the Federal Reserve purchases assets, it *creates* money—out of thin air—to make the purchase, and, in that way, "injects" money into the "economy." When the Federal Reserve sells assets, it takes money out of the "economy." In this way, the Federal Reserve is thought to regulate the money supply. Of course, this is only the tip of the proverbial iceberg. The banks, through a process they call "fractional reserve lending," create out of nothing many times more money than does the Federal Reserve.
Federal Reserve Note	Title 12, United States Code Section 411, requires that Federal Reserve Notes "[S]hall be redeemed in lawful money on demand at the Treasury Department of the United States, in the city of Washington, District of Columbia, or at any Federal Reserve bank." Thus, it was never anticipated that Federal Reserve Notes *per se* would be "lawful money." Today, Federal Reserve Notes are not *bona fide* notes at all, but tokens, a material misrepresentation.

Term	Meaning
Fiat Money	Arbitrary money. The notion of fiat money is that something that is nearly worthless is somehow endowed with "value" along with "legal tender," a.k.a. "forced tender" status. A piece of paper with ink on it, such as a Federal Reserve "Note," is an example of fiat money.
Fiscal Policy	Government tax and spending decisions.
Floating Exchange Rates	The notion that the exchange rates between various national currencies may fluctuate.
Fractional reserve lending	Money creation by a bank (by law, only banks are allowed to engage in fractional reserve lending). Banks *create* deposits, which, with a fiat system is the equivalent of money, when they extend credit, as with a mortgage or a merger & acquisition loan.
Gold Bullion Standard	A monetary system in which money is defined in terms of gold, but the fiduciary money, i.e., the paper receipts, are redeemable only in gold bars, usually large ones. A gold bullion standard differs from a gold standard in that the bars are so valuable very few people, as a practical matter, are able to redeem into gold. Knowing this, the monetary authority and the banks can create much more money than they would be able to if ordinary people could redeem at will.

Term	Meaning
Gold Exchange Standard	Central banks accumulated shares of their international monetary reserves in the form of balances of the major national currencies— mostly British pounds sterling and U.S. dollars. In theory, they could at any time demand the conversion of these balances into gold.
Gold Standard	A monetary system where the money consists of gold coins or fiduciary money redeemable into gold coins on demand.
Illiquid Asset	An asset that can not be easily and quickly be exchanged for cash, such as real estate.
International Monetary System	The conditions under which different national currencies are exchanged for one another. It was debasement of national coinage that created a need for an international monetary system that would be equitable to all, e.g., the gold standard.
Investing	Instead of hoarding accumulated wealth, provided one's property is thought to be protected by property rights and by the Rule of Law, one tends to employ accumulated wealth in productive enterprise: either physical capital, such as plant or equipment, or intellectual capital.

Term	Meaning
Legal tender	A.k.a. "forced tender," the notion that something is money and has value by virtue of law. Legal tender is inconsistent with the principles of a free market and is the indicia of a tyranny.
Lender of last resort	The word "lender" is a misnomer. The "lender of last resort" is almost always a central bank. In the event that financial assets, e.g., loans, mortgages, stocks, real estate, owned by mostly banks (although brokerage houses, insurance companies, and others now fall under the subsidy umbrella) become impaired, then the Federal Reserve is empowered to create money *without limit* to purchase these impaired assets from financial institutions.
Losses	Signals of inefficient allocation of resources in a free market.
Medium of exchange	An intermediate good, e.g., a commodity, used to facilitate barter. It has long been recognized that the best medium of exchange serves also as a so-called "store of value," to be used for future payment. Fiat money, the kind we have now, does not serve this function well.
Monetary Policy	Interest rate manipulation, usually by a central bank.

Term	Meaning
Money	The stuff we trade with, i.e., a medium of exchange. Ideally it is a standard of value and a store of purchasing power for future use. General acceptability is what distinguishes money from other commodities. It is used primarily for exchange and not as a final product. Lesser, but important characteristics are durability, fungibility, divisibility, and relative scarcity. Also, new supply should not appreciably change its relative value compared to other things. Because gold has almost fifty years' of production supply above ground, the only commodity with such a large amount of above-ground inventory, it is uniquely qualified as money.
Money substitute	When the agreed upon money is a commodity, sometimes people use a proxy, e.g., paper that is redeemable on demand into the commodity, for convenience instead of transporting the commodity. The paper is thus a "money substitute." The paper "money" *per se* is not money, but, rather, a promise to pay money, as with a "promissory note," a.k.a., a "note."
Pound Sterling	A weight of silver out of which were minted 240 silver pennies. As originally constituted, all monetary units were defined as a weight of metal.

Term	Meaning
Private Currency	The notion that anyone could issue his own currency. Of course, private currency would not have Legal Tender status. This means that (in a free market) it would only circulate only if people perceived that it had value that would not change. If the issuer were to debase his currency, then people would reject it, and the issuer would be out of business.
Profits	Signals of efficient allocation of resources in a free market.
Regulations	Signals of systemic flaws, i.e., flaws in the system require regulation in order to hopefully contain and mute ill-effects of those flaws.
Shilling	Twelve silver pennies. Twenty shillings, therefore, equaled one pound.
Smithsonian Agreement	Proclaimed by President Nixon in December 1971 as the "greatest monetary agreement in the history of the world," countries promised to maintain fixed exchange rates, but without a role for gold. Soon thereafter, the Smithsonian Agreement collapsed.
Special Drawing Rights	Gold-value guaranteed reserve claims on the International Monetary Fund (IMF). Really just a bunch of gobbledy gook to give the illusion that there was an asset when there was none.

Term	Meaning
Specie	Money in coin, usually gold or silver.
Systemic Risk	The risk that the entire financial system will collapse, i.e., "system risk."
Trade Balance	For a particular country, the "trade balance" equals the sum value of its exports minus the sum value of its imports.
Wealth	What you have left after you consume what you produce. Wealth is accumulated productive assets, both tangible and intangible. It takes work to produce wealth. Fiat money and paper securities denominated in fiat money, on the other hand, do not require any work to produce. For example, how much more work is involved in creating a $100 bill as compared to a $1 bill? The dictionary definition of wealth is: "Abundance of valuable material possessions or recourses; abundant supply; profusion; all property that has a money value or an exchangeable value; all material objects that have economic utility; especially the stock of useful goods having economic value in existence at any one time <national>." Fiat money does not fall within that definition.[1]

---

[1] *Webster's Ninth New Collegiate Dictionary*, 1983, Merriam-Webster, Inc. Springfield, Massachusetts, USA, page 1335.

Reading List

In the last century, everyone knew about the "money issue." Major political campaigns were fought over it from the time of the Revolution up until the Presidential election of 1896—William (pro-Gold) McKinley vs. William Jennings (pro-Silver/"Cross of Gold") Bryan. McKinley—and gold—won, and the matter was thought to have been settled. As more fully explained in FAME's Fight for Honest Monetary Weights and Measures brochure, even when President Roosevelt arbitrarily seized all of our citizens gold in 1933, unilaterally erasing the gold clause from all existing contracts and reneging on the Government's promise to redeem its obligations in gold, that evening, in one of his famous "Fireside Chats," he flatly stated "This currency is not fiat currency."

Since that time, Americans and others all over the world have been dumbed down on the money issue. Not only do the "Baby Boomers" know little of these matters, but their children, "Generation X," have never even heard the phrase "fiat money." There is a burning need to bring people up the learning curve about the money issue. Otherwise, when our fraudulent fiat monetary system collapses, the blame will be placed on scapegoats, as is now occurring all over the world: "crony capitalists" in East Asia; "currency speculators" in Indonesia; and "The Jews" in Malaysia.

The publications listed below are a particularly good place to start. Most are easy-to-read monographs, some of which appear full text either in html or in pdf format on the FAME website (www.FAME.org). Those by Mr. Griffin and Dr. Rothbard are full length books. While FAME maintains and will in the future display a bibliography containing hundreds of sources (along with full text on more than 100), those listed below are among the best and we recommend that you start with these. If you have any questions or comments about any of the material contained therein, please don't hesitate to write us.

Author	Title; where found
Fekete, Antal E.	"Whither Gold"; (fame.org)
Griffin, Edward	*The Creature from Jekyll Island: A Second Look at the Federal Reserve*
Parks, Lawrence M.	"The Oncoming Monetary Collapse and the Fight for Honest Money"; (fame.org)
Parks, Lawrence M.	"What the President Should Know about our Monetary System" ; (fame.org)
Paterson, Isabel B.	"Why Real Money is Indispensable" ; (fame.org)
Rothbard, Murray N.	*The Case Against The Fed*
Vieira, Jr., Edwin	"Approaching the Crossroads: The American System Or The Corporative State?"; (fame.org)
Vieira, Jr., Edwin	"Constitutional Authority Of The States And The President To Intervene On Behalf Of Sound Money"; (fame.org)
Vieira, Jr., Edwin	"The Constitutional Imperative In Reform Of The Monetary & Banking System"; (fame.org)
Vieira, Jr., Edwin	"The Forgotten Role Of The Constitution In Monetary Law"; (fame.org)
Vieira, Jr., Edwin	"To Regulate The Value Of Money: Analysis Of Power Of Government To Create And Set A Value Of Money"
Vieira, Jr., Edwin	"What Is A "Dollar"? An Historical Analysis Of The Fundamental Question In Monetary Policy"; (fame.org)
Vieira, Jr., Edwin	"Why Does The United States Need Constitutional Money?"; (fame.org)

Notable Quotations:

George Bernard Shaw	"You have to choose [as a voter] between trusting to the natural stability of gold and the natural stability of the honesty and intelligence of the members of the Government. And, with due respect for these gentlemen, I advise you, as long as the Capitalist system lasts, to vote for gold."
Voltaire (1694-1778)	"Paper money eventually returns to its intrinsic value: zero."
Daniel Webster, speech in the Senate, 1833	"We are in danger of being overwhelmed with irredeemable paper, mere paper, representing not gold nor silver; no sir, representing nothing but broken promises, bad faith, bankrupt corporations, cheated creditors and a ruined people."
Thomas Jefferson to John Taylor, 1816	"I sincerely believe ... that banking establishments are more dangerous than standing armies, and that the principle of spending money to be paid by posterity under the name of funding is but swindling futurity on a large scale."
Daniel Webster	"Of all the contrivances for cheating the laboring classes of mankind, none has been more effective than that which deludes them with paper money."
St. Louis Federal Reserve Bank, Review, Nov. 1975, p.22	"The decrease in purchasing power incurred by holders of money due to inflation imparts gains to the issuers of money--."++

Federal Reserve Bank, New York : *The Story of Banks*, p.5.	"Because of 'fractional' reserve system, banks, as a whole, can expand our money supply several times, by making loans and investments."++
Federal Reserve Bank of Philadelphia, *Gold*, p. 10	"Without the confidence factor, many believe a paper money system is liable to collapse eventually."++
Federal reserve Bank of New York, *I Bet You Thought*, p.19	"Commercial banks create checkbook money whenever they grant a loan, simply by adding new deposit dollars in accounts on their books in exchange for a borrower's IOU."++
Federal Reserve Bank of Chicago, *Modern Money Mechanics*, p.3	"The actual process of money creation takes place in commercial banks. As noted earlier, demand liabilities of commercial banks are money."++
U.S. Supreme Court, Craig v. Missouri, 4 Peters 410.	"Emitting bills of credit, or the creation of money by private corporations, is what is expressly forbidden by Article 1, Section 10 of the U.S. Constitution."++
James A. Garfield	"Whoever controls the volume of money in any country is absolute master of all industry and commerce."++
Frederic Bastiat, *The Law*	"When plunder becomes a way of life for a group of men living together in society, they create for themselves in the course of time a legal system that authorizes it and a moral code that glorifies it."++
Irving Fisher, *100% Money*	"Thus, our national circulating medium is now at the mercy of loan transactions of banks, which lend, not money, but promises to supply money they do not possess."++

John Maynard Keynes, *The Economic Consequences of the Peace,* 1920, page 240

"If, however, a government refrains from regulations and allows matters to take their course, essential commodities soon attain a level of price out of the reach of all but the rich, the worthlessness of the money becomes apparent, and the fraud upon the public can be concealed no longer."

John Maynard Keynes, *The Economic Consequences of the Peace*, 1920, page 235ff

"Lenin is said to have declared that the best way to destroy the Capitalistic System was to debauch the currency. . . Lenin was certainly right. There is no subtler, no surer means of overturning the existing basis of society than to debauch the currency. The process engages all the hidden forces of economic law on the side of destruction, and does it in a manner which not one man in a million can diagnose."

Ralph M. Hawtrey, former Secretary of Treasury, England

"Banks lend by creating credit. They create the means of payment out of nothing."++

Robert H. Hemphill, former credit manager, Federal Reserve Bank of Atlanta

"Money is the most important subject intellectual persons can investigate and reflect upon. It is so important that our present civilization may collapse unless it is widely understood and its defects remedied very soon."++

Sir Josiah Stamp, former President, Bank of England

"Bankers own the earth. Take it away from them, but leave them the power to create money and control credit, and with a flick of a pen they will create enough to buy it back."++

Rt. Hon. Reginald McKenna, former Chancellor of Exchequer, England	"Those who create and issue money and credit direct the policies of government and hold in the hollow of their hands the destiny of the people."++
John Adams, letter to Thomas Jefferson	"All the perplexities, confusion and distresses in America arise not from defects in the constitution or confederation, nor from want of honor or virtue, as much from downright ignorance of the nature of coin, credit, and circulation."++
Wm. Jennings Bryan	"Money power denounces, as public enemies, all who question its methods or throw light upon its crimes."++
George Washington, in letter to J. Bowen, Rhode Island, Jan. 9, 1787	"Paper money has had the effect in your state that it will ever have, to ruin commerce, oppress the honest, and open the door to every species of fraud and injustice."++
George Bancroft, *A Plea for the Constitution* (1886)	"Madison, agreeing with the journal of the convention, records that the grant of power to emit bills of credit was refused by a majority of more than four to one. The evidence is perfect; no power to emit paper money was granted to the legislature of the United States."++
Article One, Section Ten, *United States Constitution*	"No state shall emit bills of credit, make any thing but gold and silver coin a tender in payment of debts, coin money---."++
John C. Calhoun, Speech 5/27/1836	"A power has risen up in the government greater than the people themselves, consisting of many and various powerful interest, combined in one mass; and held together by the cohesive power of the vast surplus in banks."

Andrew Jackson: To delegation of bankers discussing the Bank Renewal Bill, 1832	"You are a den of vipers and thieves. I intend to rout you out, and by the eternal God, I will rout you out."
United States Treasury Secretary Woodin, 3/7/33	"Where would we be if we had I.O.U.'s scrip and certificates floating all around the country?" Instead he decided to "issue currency against the sound assets of the banks. [As opposed to issuing currency against gold.] The Federal Reserve Act lets us print all we'll need. And it won't frighten the people. *It won't look like stage money. It'll be money that looks like real money.*" [Emphasis added.] (Source: 'Closed for the Holiday: The Bank Holiday of 1933', p20 - Federal Reserve Bank of Boston).
John Kenneth Galbraith	"The study of money, above all other fields in economics, is one in which complexity is used to disguise truth or to evade truth, not to reveal it." *Money: Whence it came, where it went* - 1975, p15.
John Kenneth Galbraith	"The process by which banks create money is so simple that the mind is repelled." *Money: Whence it came, where it went* - 1975, p29.
Senator Carter Glass, Author of the Banking Act of 1933	"Is there any reason why the American people should be taxed to guarantee the debts of banks, any more than they should be taxed to guarantee the debts of other institutions, including merchants, the industries, and the mills of the country?"

++ This quotation was compiled by Dr. Paul Hein in his book *All Work and No Pay: Life Saving Lessons in Modern Money (*full text on www.fame.org)*

About FAME

The Foundation for the Advancement of Monetary Education (FAME) is a 501(c)(3) public foundation whose mission is to educate people about the benefits of honest monetary weights and measures, as opposed to arbitrary—and fraudulent—(fiat) money which all of us are compelled to use.

The Danger From our Fraudulent Fiat Money:

- Corruption of the political process and the loss of representative government;
- Concentration of wealth in fewer hands;
- Loss of savings and pensions for ordinary people;
- Loss of jobs for ordinary people;
- Collapse of our economic system along with mass hardship and suffering;
- Social unrest and discrediting government;
- A change in the basic form of government, possibly to tyranny.

Presently, ordinary people have few ways to get authoritative information about the perils of fiat money and how they are being defrauded by it. FAME distributes and makes known that information in ways that ordinary people can relate to.

Honest Monetary Weights and Measures—which is almost always gold-as-money—is the solution because it:

- Is the principal form of preserving wealth—pensions and savings—for future needs;
- Protects property rights of people who produce wealth— primarily working people;
- Causes real wages to be higher;
- Facilitates real economic growth;
- Keeps prices stable and/or gently declining;
- Encourages saving and thrift;
- Helps keep jobs secure;
- Increases the number of good-paying manufacturing jobs;

- Discourages debt;
- Eliminates great booms and busts, as with the Great Depression;
- Reduces the likelihood of war;
- Makes for a stronger national defense capability;
- Enables social mobility;
- Makes it more likely that the people who produce wealth will be able to keep it.

FAME is particularly oriented toward working people and seniors because they are the principal victims of the fiat money fraud. As paper-ticket-token money, as we have in the U.S., melts all around the world, including in Russia, Malaysia, the Philippines, Indonesia, South Korea, Brazil, Ecuador, Mexico and elsewhere, rich people become less rich and professional people earn less. Working people, however, lose everything. They lose their savings, their pensions, and their jobs. The suffering is palpable. It is our expectation that by helping to lay the intellectual groundwork for a return to an honest monetary system, we can help preclude and ameliorate that suffering.

People should also be mindful that an implosion of our monetary system could very likely result in significant backlash. Recently I reread John Maynard Keynes' remarkable *The Economic Consequence of Peace*, which he wrote in 1919. As some may recall, Keynes had been an official representative at the Paris Peace Conference and deputy for the Chancellor of the Exchequer on the Supreme Economic Council after World War I. This book was his critical review of the resulting Peace of Versailles Treaty.

At one point, he wrote about the suffering in Germany and Austria, partially a result of the creation of too much paper-ticket money by the authorities, which he called a "fraud upon the people." There was a relatively small amount of gold backing the German and Austrian currencies, and the French wanted to seize it as part of the reparations. Contemplating the disruption of what Keynes called the "delicate and immensely complicated organization" of commercial relationships and the continuing economic chaos, he wrote fateful lines (some small paraphrasing by me):

112

"But who can say how much is endurable, or in what direction men will seek at last to escape from their misfortunes? Men will not always die quietly. For starvation, which brings to some lethargy and a helpless despair, drives other temperaments to the nervous instability of hysteria and to a mad despair. *Some will seek revenge...*" [Emphasis added.]

"The sight of this arbitrary rearrangement of riches strikes not only at security, but at confidence in the equity of the existing distribution of wealth. Those to whom the system brings windfalls, beyond their deserts and even beyond their expectations or desires, become profiteers, who are the object of the hatred of the bourgeoisie, whom the inflationism has impoverished, not less than of the proletariat."

Although Keynes penned these lines more than 80 years ago, they are still relevant today. It is urgent that citizens of good will do whatever possible to preclude that ordinary people do not lose their savings, their pensions, and their jobs because of what is, in essence, a giant monetary fraud.

Honest Monetary Weights and Measures is the Choice of Ordinary People:

Whenever Americans have had the chance to choose the medium of exchange, they have always chosen gold- and/or silver-as-money. An honest monetary system has competition: fiat money. The creators of fiat money—banks and central banks—despite their vastly inferior product, have succeeded because of coercion, misrepresentation and nondisclosure, and also in part because proponents of honest monetary weights and measures have left the playing field. They have failed to promote the benefits of an honest system, and they have failed to expose the fiat money fraud.

We believe that once the facts are known, people will once again insist upon honest monetary weights and measures. (There are compelling reasons why the commodity money of choice is gold-as-money. These reasons are more fully discussed in various publications included in the FAME website. See, especially an Interview with Lawrence Parks, FAME's Executive Director. However, FAME's mission is just educational. If, after learning the facts, people wish to use something other than gold-as-money as the medium of exchange, that should be their choice.) To put this another way, we are in favor of a fully-informed electorate and participatory democracy.

FAME's Strategy:

FAME promotes the benefits of honest monetary weights and measures while challenging the coercion, misrepresentation and nondisclosure (fraud) that make fiat money possible. This strategy recognizes that in America the media sets the agenda. As people begin to be concerned about the public policy issues associated with our fraudulent fiat money, the media will perceive that money is an issue, and politicians will begin to address it. The money issue will become self-sustaining. Emphasis will be placed on the following public policy issues:

- Corruption of the political process by campaign "contributions" from the financial sector and from large corporations with money created out of nothing, whereas ordinary people have to work for the money they contribute;
- Concentration of wealth in fewer hands;
- Wealth transfer from ordinary people to the banking system and other segments of the financial sector;
- The monopoly that the banking system, especially commercial banks, has on creating fiat money along with special privileges that no other segment of society enjoys (the concepts of a legal monopoly and "special privilege" are repugnant to the American sense);
- Systemic risk that results from the special privileges and guarantees given to the banking system that encourages it to take inordinate risk that its principals would not take if their own money were at stake. This puts ordinary people, who do not share in the rewards of the banking system's risk taking, in

danger that there will be an implosion of our economic system along with massive unemployment, loss of savings, and loss of pensions.

FAME's Commitment and Specific Program:

As a not-for-profit foundation dedicated to full and honest disclosure about the perils of our fraudulent fiat money monetary system and the benefits of honest monetary weights and measures, FAME is uniquely positioned to execute this strategy. FAME's principals have the knowledge, ability, strategic relationships, emotional commitment, drive, and the enabling vision to achieve an honest system.

We seek two immediate actions:

- Repeal of the legal tender, a.k.a. "forced tender," laws; and,

- An end to the misrepresentation—which is what helps make it a fraud—of our money as being "Federal Reserve Notes." We want them to be relabeled what they really are: "Federal Reserve Tokens."

The Right Thing to Do:

People who want the benefits of living in a free society, and who believe in the heritage of the American ideals as set forth in the *Declaration*, should join the fight for honest monetary weights and measures because:

- It is best for ourselves;
- It is best for our families;
- It is best for future generations;
- It is best for our country;
- It is based on truth; and, most important,
- Joining the Fight for Honest Monetary Weights and Measures is the right thing to do.

☑ *YES! I Want to Join the Fight for Honest Monetary Weights & Measures*

JOIN THE FIGHT FOR HONEST MONETARY WEIGHTS & MEASURES

My fully tax-deductible contribution is:

□ $2,500   □ $1,000   □ $500   □ $250   □ $100   □ $50   □ $25   □ other _____

Please charge my:

□ check enclosed □ Visa   □ Mastercard   □ American Express

Credit Card Number

Expiration

Signature

FAME
Foundation for the Advancement of Monetary Education, 501(c)(3)
Box 625, FDR Station, New York, NY 10150-0625
Phone (212) 818-1206 • Fax (212) 754-6543
E-mail: Join@FAME.org

Order copies of this book

Send me _____ copy(s) of this book

	Books	Shipping	Total
1 copy	$12.95	$1.50	$14.45
5 copies	$60.00	$5.00	$65.00
10 copies	$110.00	$8.00	$118.00
25 copies	$250.00	$20.00	$270.00
50 copies	$450.00	$30.00	$480.00
100 copies	$800.00	$50.00	$850.00

Name _____

Address _____

City _____ State _____ Zip _____

Telephone_____ e-mail:_____

My check payable to FAME is enclosed _____

Charge my: Visa_____ Mastercard _____ Amex _____

Account # _____ Exp. Date_____

Signature _____

Send to: FAME, Box 625, FDR Station, New York, NY 10150

www.fame.org

www.ingramcontent.com/pod-product-compliance
Lightning Source LLC
Chambersburg PA
CBHW031944190326
41519CB00007B/651